The
Little DOS 5
Book

Kay Yarborough Nelson

Peachpit Press
Berkeley, California

The Little DOS 5 Book
Kay Yarborough Nelson

Peachpit Press, Inc.
2414 Sixth St.
Berkeley, CA 94710
(415) 527-8555
(415) 524-9775 (fax)

Cover design: Ted Mader + Associates (TMA)
Cover illustration: Lynn Dougherty, TMA

ISBN 0-938151-43-6

0 9 8 7 6 5 4 3 2 1
Printed and bound in the United States of America

For Wanda
my new sister-in-law
Now you have no excuse for not "doing" computers.

Contents

Introduction

DOS—your computer's disk operating system—has some pretty impressive capabilities, but most of us don't need to know everything there is to know about them. All we do is day-to-day chores such as formatting disks, copying files and disks, deleting and renaming files, and things like that. And that's what this book concentrates on: helping you do those daily jobs and giving you some tips you can use to speed them up or straighten them out. You can also grab this book when you get stuck and don't know what to do next; it won't take up much room on your desk.

If you've never used a computer before, you'll find an introduction to some of its mysteries in Chapter 1 (like where the power switch is and which disk drive is which). You can skip that chapter if you know all that already. Chapter 2 will give you a guided tour of DOS 5's new graphic interface, called the Shell, so that you can get an idea of how to use it and what it can do. Then the book will discuss, in short chapters, the kinds of skills and topics you need to know more about so that you can actually do productive work with your computer without having to read some fat book that was really written for programmers.

This book assumes that you'll want to use the Shell for the things that are easiest to do with the Shell. For example, you can rename directories with the Shell; you can't do that at the command line! You can also start a program by double-clicking on it. And you can type the first few characters of a file's name to immediately go to it

Some things you can't do in the Shell, though, and you have to use the command line (or the Run command). You can look up all the DOS commands, complete with everyday examples of how you'd use them, in the back of the book.

Why DOS 5?

There are really two basic reasons to switch to DOS 5. If you're running Microsoft Windows, DOS 5 will give you more memory. (Windows is a memory hog and wants as much as it can get for itself and its programs.) If you're not running Windows, DOS 5 will give you just about the same features that Windows does, even if your computer is an old XT clone. You just won't be able to cut and paste between programs like you can in Windows.

DOS 5 is a big improvement over whatever version of DOS you've been using. In addition to the easy-to-use Shell, which gives you a graphical interface and the ability to point and click with a mouse, it takes up a lot less room in memory, so you can use that memory for your other programs. And because of the way DOS 5 manages memory, you can have several programs in memory and switch between them with a new feature called the Task Swapper.

You also get a lot of neat new utilities with DOS 5, like an Undelete command that lets you retrieve files you've deleted by mistake, a Quick Format command that will erase a used disk in 10 seconds or less, online help, and a full-screen text editor.

Try it; you'll like it.

Acknowledgments

Many thanks to Matt Kim, for formatting the book in Page-Maker. Special thanks also to editor Harry Henderson, himself a DOS expert, who took time from writing his DOS book to review this one. The book's original design was Robin Williams' for her *Little Mac Book*, and Olav Martin Kvern at Aldus redesigned it. Text is Adobe Systems' ITC New Baskerville, and headings are Futura Book. Screen shots were taken with HiJaak from Inset Systems.

DOS: The Basic Basics

"Pay no attention to the little man behind the curtain!"

FRANK MORGAN as the Wizard in MGM's
The Wizard of Oz (1939).

DOS is your computer's operating system. Without it, your computer and your favorite programs, like Lotus 1-2-3, WordPerfect, and even Windows wouldn't run. DOS, which stands for Disk Operating System, is the little man behind the curtain, controlling everything. And unfortunately, we're not in Oz, and you do have to pay some attention to it. Some, but hopefully not a lot.

If DOS isn't already on your computer, you'll need to install it. How can you tell whether it's there or not? Turn on your computer. The ON switch is probably on the right side or on the front. It's usually red. You may also need to switch on the power to your monitor, or video screen. That control is normally under the front edge of the monitor.

The Command Line

OK, does the computer start (it may take a minute to start up, or "boot") and do you see an A> or C>? Or something that begins with A:\> or C:\> or maybe even D:\>? That's called the **DOS prompt,** and it indicates that DOS is waiting for you to type a command there (that's why it's also called the **command line**). If you see the C:\> (or one of the variations), DOS is there. Check to see what version it is by typing *ver* and pressing Enter (that funny-looking key on the right side of the keyboard; it may just be labeled with a bent arrow on it). If you're not running version 5 (or if you're not running DOS at all), go to the appendix, which will tell you how to install DOS 5.

The Shell

You may instead see a screen like this one when your computer starts.

▶ **Tip:** *You can use DOS either with the Shell or with the command line.*

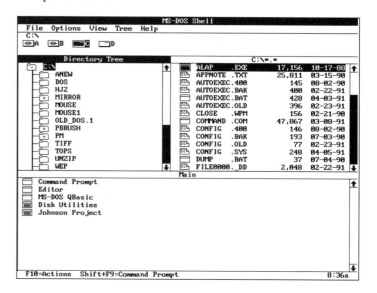

▶ **Tip:** *To switch from the Shell to the command line, press Shift-F9. To switch back from the command line to the Shell, type* exit *and press Enter.*

This is called the **Shell**. DOS 5 may have been set up to show you this screen when it was installed. The Shell lets you pick and choose from menus instead of having to remember the special commands for everything you do, so it's a lot easier to use than giving DOS direct commands.

To see the Shell if it's not showing, type *dosshell* at the DOS prompt and press Enter.

When you set up DOS 5, there's an option for whether you want the Shell to start automatically or not. But if you've already set up DOS, you don't have to set it up again to do this. If you want the Shell to come up when you start your computer, see Chapter 10.

DOS Versions

As you can tell from its name, DOS 5 is the latest in a long series of DOS's. What's the difference? Well, anything earlier than version 3.3 is pretty useless if you've got a hard disk, and you probably do. Version 3.3 was designed to handle large hard disks, whereas the earlier versions of DOS weren't. Version 4 added a shell feature, much like the DOS 5 interface, but it took up so much memory that a lot of people didn't want to use it. DOS 5 was improved to take up less memory and also give you more features, like being able to switch between programs quickly, get online help, get files and directories back if you accidentally erase them, search for the particular file you're looking for, and unformat disks and do quick formats. If you run Microsoft Windows, you'll appreciate how little memory DOS 5 takes up, too.

In fact, DOS 5 is quite similar to Windows. It gives you a graphical interface with icons (small pictorial representations of what you see on the screen) and menus that you can use with or without a mouse. Also, because of the more efficient way DOS 5 manages memory, you can have several programs running and switch between them by pressing a "hot key."

The DOS 5 Shell is the most noticeable improvement to DOS. You'll take a guided tour of the Shell in the next chapter so that you can get an idea of what it can do. But first, you need some basic skills so that you can "talk" to DOS.

The Keyboard

Because a lot of what you do with DOS is done with the keyboard, let's take a quick look at some of those funny keys.

The Enter Key

The most important one is the **Enter key**. As you saw earlier, it's the weird-looking key on the right side of your keyboard. It's probably gray. It may be labeled Return. We'll call it the Enter key because you use it to *enter* commands. DOS can't read what you've typed until you press Enter.

The Backspace Key

▶ **Tip:** *You can also delete text with the Del key.*

The second most important key is the **Backspace key**. It's just above the Enter key, and it has a backward-pointing arrow on it. It may or may not be labeled Backspace, but that's what it is. You use it to correct mistakes. When you press Backspace, you erase the character to the left of the cursor (the blinking underline). So if you make a mistake in typing before you press Enter, just press Backspace, erase it, and correct it. You'll see more about entering commands later in the book.

The Function Keys

The gray keys labeled F1 through F10 (you may have more than those, depending on what keyboard you have) are either on the left side of the keyboard or across the top.

The Numeric Keypad

▶ **Tip:** *If you see an instruction to use the F1 key, press the gray F1 key; don't type f and 1.*

Over on the far-right side of your keyboard is an arrangement of number keys that may also have arrows on them. That's the **numeric keypad**. It's designed to be used to enter numbers quickly, like a ten-key calculator. When Num Lock is on (you toggle it on and off by pressing the Num Lock key) and you press those number keys, you get numbers. When Num Lock's off, those keys move the cursor. You may have a light on your keyboard that comes on when Num Lock is on, or you may not. On some keyboards, Num Lock comes on when you start your computer.

You'll also see Home and End on a couple of these keys. You can use them to go to the beginning and end of a list in DOS 5. The keys marked PgUp and PgDn also move you through lists, one screen at a time.

The Cursor Keys

▶ **Tip:** *The cursor isn't the same as the prompt. The cursor is a small blinking underline that shows you where you are on a line.*

If you have an older keyboard, you'll need to use the numeric keypad (with Num Lock off) to move the cursor. Look closely, and you'll see arrows on the 4, 8, 6, and 2 keys. They represent the direction the cursor will go when you press that key. To move the cursor down one line, you'd press 2, and so forth.

If you've got a newer keyboard, there'll be **cursor keys** at the bottom of the keyboard on the right. They're arranged in an upside-down T formation. They'll move the cursor so that you don't have to worry about whether Num Lock is on or not.

There are a lot of other keys, aren't there? Here are a few more you may need to know about:

- The **Esc key**, on the upper-left side of the keyboard, will cancel a command.

- The **Tab key**, just under the Esc key, moves the cursor one tab space. You also use it to move from area to area in the Shell. It may not be marked Tab but may have two arrows on it, or it may have Tab and the two arrows.

- The **Ctrl key** is used in combination with other keys. You'll probably see it represented like this: Ctrl-C. That means "press Ctrl and C at the same time." Pressing Ctrl-C is like pressing Esc; it bails you out of whatever's going on.

- The **Shift key** shifts you from lowercase to uppercase. DOS doesn't care which you use, so you can use either, or a combination of both.

- The **Print Screen key** (it may be marked Prt Sc) will send a copy of what's on your screen (called a screen dump) to your printer. Be sure to turn your printer on first.

- The **Alt key**, just under the Shift key, works like the Ctrl key: you press it in combination with other keys. When you see Alt-R, for example, press Alt and R and the same time.

- The **Pause** or **Break key** (you may have both of these, or just one) will stop whatever your computer's doing. If you don't have a Pause key, you can press Ctrl and Num Lock at the same time.

Other Keys

▶ **Tip:** *DOS doesn't care whether you use uppercase or lowercase.*

▶ **Tip:** *To restart your computer without actually turning the power off, press Ctrl, Alt, and Del, all at the same time. This is usually represented as Ctrl-Alt-Del.*

You may or may not have a **mouse**. If I were you, I'd get one. Having a mouse makes DOS and most of your programs a lot more fun to use. If you're not sure whether you have a mouse, look for a rectangular object about the size of a cigarette pack attached by a cord to your computer. Technically, it's a pointing device that controls the position of the pointer on the screen. As you move the mouse on the desktop, the pointer moves on the screen.

The Mouse

▶ **Tip:** *If you want to use a mouse, you'll need to have installed it according to the directions that came with it.*

In DOS, the mouse only works when you're running the Shell or Editor, so we'll wait for the guided tour of the DOS Shell to practice your mouse skills.

There are a couple of other things you may need to know about. One is about your disk drives and where they are. Why are they important? Think about it. All the programs you buy come on floppy disks, and they have to get onto your hard disk in some way. That's through your floppy disk drive.

Disk Drives

Your computer has at least one floppy disk drive. The main one's called drive A. If you have two floppy disk drives, drive A's the one on the left. If one floppy disk drive is above the other, drive A is usually the one on the top.

The second floppy disk drive, if you've got one, is called drive B. Drive C is your hard disk. If you have more than one hard disk, or if you've divided a great big hard disk into smaller sections called partitions, the next drive's drive D, and so on.

▶ **Tip:** *The Disks chapter has more information about floppy disks.*

Disk drives come in two sizes, one for 5.25-inch floppy disks and one for 3.5-inch floppy disks (which aren't very floppy; they're the little hard plastic ones). The little ones hold more data. And because they're harder, they're less likely to get damaged. They're also more expensive than the bigger ones. But you have to have a 3.5-inch disk drive to use them, and some computers (like the IBM XT) don't have that kind of drive as standard equipment. It's nicest when you have both types of drives—then you can use both kinds of disks.

Inserting Disks

When you put a disk in your floppy disk drive, slide it in with the label facing up and the little oval going into the drive first (if it's a 5.25-inch disk) or the metal shutter going into the drive first (if it's a 3.5-inch disk). Match the sizes to the slots: don't try to put one of the little 3.5-inch disks into a big 5.25-inch slot.

▶ **Tip:** *Store your floppy disks in a safe place that's relatively cool and dry. Keep them away from magnets! Magnets destroy whatever's on a disk.*

Then make sure you close the drive door, if you're using a 5.25-inch disk. Pull the door latch down. (On a 3.5-inch drive, the door will close when you push the disk in far enough.)

You hear "memory" discussed a lot, both in terms of disks and in terms of your computer. Here's the secret: there are two kinds of memory: **disk storage** and **random-access memory (RAM).** The kind of memory that's used for storage—on floppy and hard disks—isn't the same thing as the random-access memory (RAM) that's on chips in your computer. What's stored on disks stays there, even after you turn off your computer (that is, if you don't dump a cup of coffee on the disk or crumple it up or do something else nasty to it). What's in RAM is the information your computer is actually working with. When you turn off the computer (or when the lights go out), that information's gone if it hasn't been saved (stored) on disk yet. That's why it's important to save your work frequently when you work with programs.

To understand a little about memory and storage, you need to know how these things are measured. Both of them are rated in terms of bytes (a **byte** is one character). A thousand bytes (roughly) is a **kilobyte,** which is abbreviated K. A million bytes is a **megabyte,** which is abbreviated Mb.

Most computers nowadays have at least 640K of random-access memory (RAM), but you only need 256K of it to run DOS 5. You can have much more random-access memory than this, and DOS will be happy to use it. For example, to run DOS and Windows, you'll need 2 Mb of RAM to be comfortable (and even more is better).

Floppy disks typically store between 360K to 1.44 Mb of data. Your basic plain vanilla 5.25-inch floppy disk holds 360K, for example. And your hard disk probably holds 10 or 20 Mb or so, but it might be even larger: there are even 150-Mb hard disks out there.

Now, here's the practical difference between them. The more RAM you have, the more programs you can run at once. The bigger your hard disk, the more programs and data you can store. Got it? They're two different things.

You'll find out more details about disks and storage capacities in the Disks chapter. But for now, let's get to the guided tour right away.

If you see the C:\> prompt on your screen, type *dosshell* to start the Shell. If you're already at the Shell, you're ready to begin.

Memory and Storage

A Guided Tour

Sattinger's Law: It works better if you plug it in.

ARTHUR BLOCH,
Murphy's Law, 1977

In this chapter we'll take a guided tour of the Shell so that you can quickly get familiar with it and practice the basic ways you interact with it. Start your computer so that you can follow along.

When you've got the Shell on your screen, you should see something that looks like this:

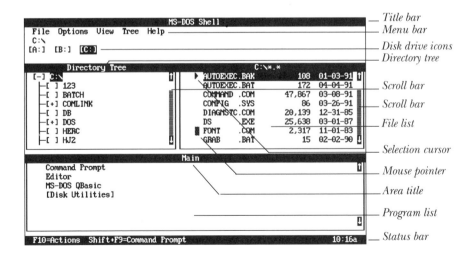

▶ **Tip:** *Go to Appendix A if you haven't installed DOS 5 yet.*

Yours will look a little different, because you'll have different files on your computer, of course. This screen is what usually appears if you haven't made any changes to the way DOS displays the Shell.

Menu Bar

At the top of the screen is the Shell **menu bar**, showing File, Options, View, Tree, and Help. If you select any of these menus, you'll see more choices.

Disk Drive Icons

Just underneath the menus are representations of your disk drives. Drive C, your hard disk, is highlighted, or displayed in reverse video. If you're looking at a graphics display, it will

Shell graphics display

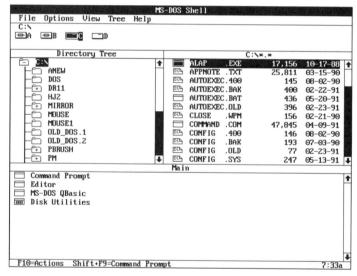

look prettier than a text screen. You'll see **icons,** or small pictorial representations, of your drives. (You'll see how to switch to a graphics display before you leave this chapter.)

Directory Tree

The next area down, called the **directory tree,** lets you see at a glance how the files on your disks are organized. Everything that's on your computer is stored as a file—spreadsheets, graphic images, programs, documents: they're all files. Here DOS is listing the files that are on drive C. Each little box—or folder icon, if you're looking at a graphics display, represents a **directory,** or a collection of files. If it has a + on it, there are more directories, called **subdirectories,** underneath it.

File List

To the right of the directory tree area is a list of all the files that are in the highlighted directory. Since only drive C is highlighted, the files listed here are the ones that are in the top-level directory of drive C. If you were to highlight another directory, you'd see a list of the files in it appear in this area, which is called (appropriately) the **file list**.

Program List

At the bottom of the screen is the **program list**. This is a list of groups of programs. When you first use DOS 5, it shows only the Main group, which contains the DOS Command Prompt, the Editor (a text editor), QBasic (a programming language), and the Disk Utilities program group, which contains several programs that let you format and copy disks, and undelete files you deleted by mistake.

Program Groups

You can add programs to the Main group and the Disk Utilities group, or even create a group of your own. Being able to create groups of programs is one of the new features in DOS 5 that makes it very much like Windows. If you use a program often, you can put it in a group along with documents that you use with it. Then you can start the program just by choosing the document you want to work with. No more "What was the name of that document?" and "Where did I save it?" or "What command do I use to start this program?" You'll see how later in the book, in the Programs chapter.

▶ **Tip:** *Instead of looking at files and programs, you can look at just files or just programs. There are quite a few different choices on the View menu. You'll see different views in the Files, Directories, and Programs chapters.*

Running Several Programs at Once

DOS 5 also lets you run several programs at once and switch between them. When a special feature called the **Task Swapper** is turned on (it's in the Options menu), the Shell screen changes to show you an active task list. You can then start programs running, and their names will appear in the task list. You can switch among them by pressing Alt-Tab. For example, you might want to have

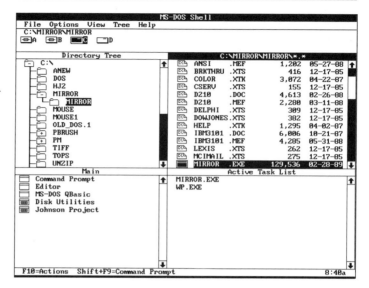

When the Task Swapper's on, you see a list of all the programs you've got running in the Active Task List.

your spreadsheet program, a graphics program, and your word processor all loaded at the same time so that you can go back and forth and check data and graphics for a document you're writing. How many programs you can run at once depends on how much memory you've got. But because of the way DOS 5 uses memory, folks, you can even do this on an XT!

The Graphic Interface

The Shell is called a **graphic interface** because it lets you interact with your computer by **selecting** items that are represented on the screen instead of remembering cryptic commands.

Selecting

▶ **Tip:** *You have to select something before you can work with it.*

To select menu items or icons, you can either use the keyboard or a mouse. It's more fun to use a mouse, so we'll look at that first. But you can use DOS 5 without a mouse. If you don't have one, skip the stuff about the mouse.

A **mouse** is a pointing device that controls the position of the pointer on the screen. If you've installed your mouse properly, according to the instructions that came with it, you should see a small arrowhead or a shaded box on the Shell's screen. As you move the mouse on the desktop, the pointer moves on the screen. Try it and see.

You can pick the mouse up! If you've pushed it all the way to the far corner of your desk and you're just about to knock over your coffee cup, just pick it up and put it down closer to you. The pointer on the screen won't move. In fact, a lot of people get in the habit of just sort of keeping the mouse in place and scooting it a little way over and over again to move the screen pointer. If you haven't used a mouse before, try moving it and watching the pointer on the screen.

You use the mouse in three basic ways: by clicking, double-clicking, and dragging.

To select an item on the screen, you can move the mouse pointer to it and **click** once with the left mouse button. Once an item's selected, it's highlighted (and there's a tiny arrow next to it, on a text screen). For example, you might click on a folder icon so that you could see the files that are in that directory.

You can also just click in any of the different areas on the Shell screen to move into that area. This is a lot faster than using the keyboard to move between the different areas of the Shell's screen.

You can **double-click** on some items to select them and start them at the same time. For example, you can double click on the name of a program to start it running. To double-click, quickly click twice with the left mouse button.

You can also double-click on a program group icon to open it, or to close it once it's open.

You can Shift-click to select files that are next to each other. Just click on the first one, and then press and hold down the Shift key and click on the last one.

You can hold down the Ctrl key while you click to select items that aren't next to each other.

Using a Mouse

▶ **Tip:** *The mouse doesn't work in DOS outside the Shell. It won't work on the command line.*

Clicking

Double-Clicking

Shift-Clicking

▶ **Tip:** *The Files chapter will have more tips about selecting files.*

Dragging

Another way to use the mouse is by **dragging.** You can move files into different directories by dragging them. To drag, put the mouse pointer on what you want to move, press and hold the left button down, and then move the mouse. The item will move with it, if it can be moved. If you don't want to move the item but make a copy of it instead and leave the original where it is, press the Ctrl key while you drag.

▶ **Tip:** *Press Ctrl and drag to copy.*

The Keyboard

You can also use DOS 5 just with the keyboard, if you don't have a mouse, or you can switch back and forth and use a mouse for some things and the keyboard for others. That's what I do, because sometimes it's easier just to keep your hand on the keyboard instead of reaching for the mouse.

Moving to Different Areas

The area you want to work in has to be active before you can work in it. To move from area to area on the screen with the keyboard, press Tab. The highlight will move, showing that the area's active. If you have a color monitor, the title bar will change color, too. Try it. Then press Shift-Tab to move the active area counterclockwise.

▶ **Tip:** *Press Tab to move from area to area with the keyboard, or click with the mouse.*

Selecting

Once you're within the area where you want to select something, you can use the arrow keys to move the highlight up or down. If you've selected a program, you can press Enter to start it; if it's a program group you've selected, you can open or close it by pressing Enter.

▶ **Tip:** *If you're using a text screen instead of a graphics screen, there'll be a little arrow in the active area. Pressing Tab moves the tiny arrow clockwise from one area to the next.*

```
┌──────Disk Utilities──────┐
│ ▦ Main                  ↑│
│ ▤ Disk Copy              │
│ ▤ Backup Fixed Disk      │
│ ▤ Restore Fixed Disk     │
│ ▤ Quick Format           │
│ ▤ Format                 │
```

Try this now. Press Tab until you move into the Main Group area. If Disk Utilities isn't highlighted there, press the down arrow key until the highlight's on Disk Utilities. Then press Enter. You should then see a list of Disk Utilities, and you could choose one of them by highlighting it and pressing Enter. Highlight Main and press Enter to go back to where you were.

The menus at the top of the screen let you perform actions on what you've selected. You can select a file and then choose Copy from the File menu, for example, to copy the file.

So what are these menus for? The commands on them let you carry out most of your everyday tasks, like copying files and disks. As you go further in the book, you'll find instructions for how to do these jobs and what to choose from the menus. In general, here's what the various menus do:

- The **File menu** lets you run programs; give DOS commands; search for a file you're looking for; delete, copy, move, and rename files; and create directories for storing files in.

- The **Options menu** lets you change things about the way DOS 5 works, like whether you want to be prompted each time you delete a file or what information you want to see about your files on the screen. It also lets you change the screen colors, if you have a color monitor, and choose whether you want text or graphics display.

- The **View menu** controls whether you're looking at files on one disk or two, and whether you're looking at lists of programs, files, or both. It also lets you tell DOS to update the screen, if you've created new files in a program.

- The **Tree menu** lets you view your computer's filing system of directories and subdirectories. You can "expand" a directory to see what subdirectories are underneath it.

- The **Help menu** lets you get help on what you're doing. You'll see more about it later in this chapter.

To select from menus, you can use either the mouse, the keyboard, or a combination of both. To select from a menu with the mouse, just click on the menu name to open it. You can then click on the item you want to select it. Try it on the File menu. Click on File; then click on Run. (You can drag to it, too. Or you can just type the letter that's underlined or highlighted, like *d* for Delete

Menus

▶ **Tip:** *Why is the shell called the Shell? Basically, because it surrounds the inner workings of your computer (the machine language part) and provides a way for you to give commands without having to use your computer's language, or use DOS commands at the command line.*

▶ **Tip:** *Press Esc to cancel a menu.*

on the File menu.) If you wanted to run a program, you'd type the command used to start it in the box that DOS shows you. Since you don't want to run a program now, click on Cancel or press Esc to get back to the regular display.

If you're using the keyboard to select from menus, press Alt (or F10) first. That selects the menu bar, even if you're in a different area of the screen. You can then use the right and left arrow keys to move to the menu you want to open and press Enter when it's highlighted.

Try this: Press Alt, press the right arrow key twice, and then press Enter to see what's on the View menu. Then press the left arrow key once to see what's on the Options menu. Press Esc to get back to the regular display.

▶ **Tip:** *Here's a neat shortcut for selecting from menus: press Alt and type the first letter of the menu's name, like Alt-F for File. Then type the underlined or highlighted letter of the command you want to use. For example, Alt-F R opens the File menu and chooses Run.*

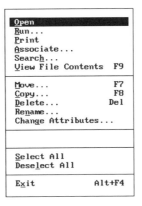

```
Open
Run...
Print
Associate...
Search...
View File Contents    F9

Move...                F7
Copy...                F8
Delete...              Del
Rename...
Change Attributes...


Select All
Deselect All

Exit               Alt+F4
```

Once the menu is displayed, you can use the down arrow key to move to the item you want and press Enter, or you can type the special letter in the command. The second way's faster.

What you see on the menus depends on what you're doing. If you've selected a file, for example, you'll see a lot more choices on the File menu that you would if no file were selected. Try this now. Select any file in the file list (on the right side of the display); then select the File menu. Aha! More choices.

Keyboard Shortcuts

Now you can see another little trick. Look at the File menu. In the second column, you'll see keys like F9 or Del listed. Those are **keyboard shortcuts** for the menu choice. For example, if you wanted to see what's in a highlighted file, you could just press F9. Back out of the File menu without choosing anything (press Esc or click somewhere else on the screen, out of the menu) and then press F9. (You may see garbage if the file you've selected isn't a text file.) Now, that's a handy thing to know about: you can take a peek at what's in a file without starting the program that created it. Press Esc to get back to the Shell screen.

Whenever you see a key listed to a menu choice, you can press it instead of using the menu system. You can also get online Help on them by choosing Keyboard from the Help menu. (You'll see more about the Help system later.)

If you see a diamond next to a menu item, that means it's active.

▶ **Tip:** *Sometimes items on a menu will be dimmed. That means you can't select that item at this time. You may have to select something else first—a file, for example.*

Dialog Boxes

If you see ... next to a menu item, it means that a **dialog box** will come up when you choose that item. If you choose Run... from the File menu, you'll see a dialog box where you can type the name of the program to run.

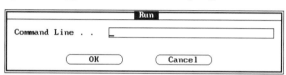

Dialog boxes let you supply extra information that DOS needs. They can also give you warnings about what you're doing.

You can just press Esc or click on Cancel to get out of a dialog box without doing anything.

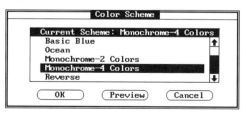

There are a lot of different kinds of dialog boxes. In some of them, you have to type **text,** like the Run dialog box. Some of them provide text that's already there, and if it's not what you want, you can type new text to replace it (just start typing; the new text will replace what's already there). For example, this dialog box assumes that you want to format a disk that's in drive A. You can just type B: to use drive B.

In others you can choose items from a **list.**

To select an item, highlight it with the arrow keys and then press Enter. If you've got a mouse, you can often just double-click on the item to select it and complete the command. This doesn't work in all dialog boxes, though.

Other kinds of dialog boxes let you choose command buttons. You can press Enter to choose OK or press Esc to select Cancel, or click with the mouse on either one. If you move from button to button with the keyboard, there'll be a tiny underline on the button that's selected. Sometimes you have to look closely to see it. You can press Enter to select it, too.

```
╔══════════════════╡ Search File ╞══════════════════╗
║                                                    ║
║  Current Directory is C:\WP51\DOCS                 ║
║                                                    ║
║  Search for. .  ▐*.*▌                              ║
║                                                    ║
║            [X] Search entire disk                  ║
║                                                    ║
║    ( OK )        ( Cancel )        ( Help )        ║
╚════════════════════════════════════════════════════╝
```

To move from button to button, press Tab or an arrow key (or just click with the mouse on the button you want).

Another kind of dialog box lets you choose only one option. The option button that's selected has a tiny black dot:

```
╔═════════════════╡ File Display Options ╞═══════════╗
║                                                     ║
║  Name:   ▐*.*▌                                      ║
║                                          Sort by:   ║
║                                                     ║
║  [ ] Display hidden/system files       ◉ Name      ║
║                                        ○ Extension  ║
║                                        ○ Date       ║
║  [ ] Descending order                  ○ Size       ║
║                                        ○ DiskOrder  ║
║                                                     ║
║     ( OK )        ( Cancel )        ( Help )        ║
╚═════════════════════════════════════════════════════╝
```

And yet another kind, called a **check box,** lets you choose several options at once (press the space bar to select these kinds of items with the keyboard):

Sometimes DOS can't display everything on the screen all at once. If that's the case, you'll see a **scroll bar** on the right of the area, like the one on the right of the directory tree area here.

Here's another place where the mouse is sometimes handier than the keyboard. To scroll the contents of the screen, you can click on the scroll arrows to move up or down one item at a time, or you can just drag the scroll box to about where you want to go. To go to the beginning of a long list, drag the scroll bar to the top. To go to the end, drag it to the bottom. Drag it to the middle to go to the middle. You get the idea.

If you're using the keyboard, you can press and hold down the up and down arrow keys to scroll, or you can use these keyboard shortcuts to move through lists:

PgUp, PgDn	To scroll one window up or down
Home	To go to the first item in a list
End	To go to the last item in a list

Scroll Bars

▶ **Tip:** *To scroll continuously with the mouse, click on one of the scroll arrows and hold the mouse button down until you see what you're looking for.*

— *Scroll bar*

— *Scroll arrow*

▶ **Tip:** *Once an area is active, you can just type the first letter of an item's name to move directly to the first item in the list that begins with that letter. Very handy if you're looking for a file or directory beginning with W.*

Customizing Your Display

Before you go any further with DOS 5, there are a couple of things you can do to customize it as you'd like it.

If you have a graphics monitor, you can choose how DOS 5 displays the Shell on your screen—whether you see icons, or whether you see just text. You'll probably want graphics. In addition, if yours is a color monitor, you can change the color scheme DOS uses.

Graphics and Text Mode

Choose Display from the Options menu to see a Screen Display Mode dialog box. What you see will depend on your system, and you may need to scroll to see more choices. Choose Preview to see how each one looks. When you see a display you like, choose OK.

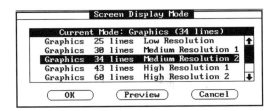

Color Scheme

▶ **Tip:** *Even if you don't have a color monitor, you can choose two or four shades in monochrome, or choose reverse video.*

DOS comes with several predefined color schemes, and if you have a color monitor, you can pick different ones by choosing Colors from the Options menu. Scroll to see them all.

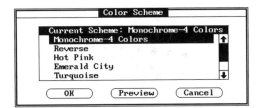

These are for a VGA monitor. Try Hot Pink for something truly garish. Emerald City's pretty wild, too. Basic Blue and Ocean are a little more restrained.

There's one other very basic skill you need before you explore DOS 5 on your own, and that's getting online help.

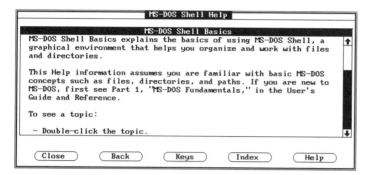

Help!

▶ **Tip:** *The first time you use Help, choose Using Help so that you can get acquainted with the kind of help that's available.*

To get help with an item that you've selected, just press F1. DOS displays a Help window with information about what you've selected. If you need more information, you can click on one of the other references that are listed at the end of the entry (if you don't have a mouse, move to them with the Tab key and press Enter to choose one).

If you don't want help on a specific item, or if you don't know what you want help on, you can use the Help menu. Just press Alt-H or click on the Help menu.

Choose Index to see a list of all the Help topics. If you choose Keyboard, you'll get a list of all the keyboard shortcuts you can use with the Shell. Choosing Commands gets you information on all the commands, and Procedures gives you instructions for how to do tasks in the Shell. Shell Basics gives you an introduction to using the Shell, and you might want to go through that now, just to review what you've learned in this chapter before you go on to the next.

▶ **Tip:** *You don't have to be in the Shell to get help. At the command line, you canget help by entering /? after the command. For example, entering* del /? *gets you help on the DELETE command. Or you can type* help, *a space, and the name of the command you want help on and then press Enter.*

Entering Commands

May all your wishes come true.

ANCIENT IRISH CURSE

DOS has a lot more commands than those that are represented in the Shell's menus. (They're all in the back of the book, in case you're interested.) The Shell just has commands for the things you do most often, like copying and moving files, formatting disks, and so on. But in the Shell you still sometimes have to fill out dialog boxes with whatever's needed to complete the command, like the new name you want a file to have, so you can't get completely avoid learning the rules you have to follow about entering commands.

You can give commands to DOS either from within the Shell (in dialog boxes) or at the command line (at the DOS prompt).

Using the Command Line

To get to the command line from the Shell, press Shift-F9 or choose Command Prompt from the Main Group. You can just double-click on it with your mouse.

To enter a DOS command on the command line, you start with the **name** of the command, followed by what you want it to work on (the **parameters**). You can then add cryptic **options** (sometimes called "switches") that let you specify how the command is to work. For example, in the command DIR A: /P, DIR is the command you're using to

▶ **Tip:** *To get back to the Shell after you've left it this way, type* exit.

tell DOS to list a directory (DIR) of the files on drive A (A:) and to pause (/P) after each screen of files.

DIR A: /P

Command   *Parameters*   *Option*

▶ **Tip:** *Neat trick: on the command line, to repeat a command that you just used, press F3.*

You'll find examples of how to enter each DOS command in the DOS Commands section in the back of this book. In particular, you'll see examples of how to use the options that let you specify just exactly how you want a task performed.

Keep a few things in mind when you enter commands on the command line:

- You enter commands at the DOS prompt (A:\>, C:\>, etc.). DOS types the A:\> or C:\>; you don't.

- You can use either caps or lowercase; DOS doesn't care which you use. I'm showing DOS commands in uppercase to distinguish them from the Shell menu commands.

▶ **Tip:** *To cancel a command you've typed before you press Enter, just press Esc.*

- If you make a mistake while typing a command, backspace over it and correct it (the Backspace key is the one with the backward arrow on it, just above the Enter key).

- You have to press Enter after you've typed the command, so that DOS can read what you typed.

▶ **Tip:** *Once a command is running, you can stop it by pressing Ctrl-C.*

If you press Enter and you've entered the command wrong, you'll get a "bad command" message. Just re-enter it. DOS is very picky about how it wants things, and you have to be exact.

You may get other messages, like "invalid directory" or "file not found." These usually mean that you didn't correctly specify the information the command needed.

Entering Commands in the Shell

You can't get away from entering commands, even in the Shell! Although you choose the command you want from a menu, often the Shell just makes it easier by giving you a dialog box that's partially been filled out with what DOS thinks you want to do. For example, if you choose Copy from the File menu, DOS assumes that you want to copy it onto your hard disk, drive C, and gives you this dialog box:

▶ **Tip:** *You can copy by pressing Ctrl and dragging files with the mouse to avoid this dialog box.*

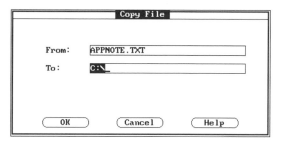

The name of the file you've highlighted has been filled in for you, and drive C and the directory you're in are filled in as the To: location. You can just type over what's being displayed, if it's not what you want. So you still have to know a few things about how to name files and such. (See the Files chapter for more on this.)

▶ **Tip:** *You can use either uppercase or lowercase to enter text in the Shell's dialog boxes. It doesn't matter which.*

You can choose Run from the File menu and give a DOS command there. You can run any program that way, too. (A DOS command is actually just a little program.) For example, if you wanted to delete a file named DOS.DOC, you could choose Run and enter the command DEL DOS.DOC in the Run dialog box and click OK.Or if you wanted to run WordPerfect, you could just type *wp* there.

Running DOS Commands with the Shell

```
┌─────────────────────── Run ───────────────────────┐
│                                                    │
│  Command Line . .  │del dos.doc_            │     │
│                                                    │
│        ( OK )              ( Cancel )              │
└────────────────────────────────────────────────────┘
```

DOS will delete the file and ask you to press any key to return to the Shell. You can do this with the other DOS commands, too.

You can also choose Command Prompt from the Main group. This is the same as pressing Shift-F9, which takes you out to the command line until you type *exit* and press Enter to return to the Shell. This is the best way to run several DOS commands using the command line.

▶ **Tip:** *This is a fast way to give a single DOS command without actually going out to the command line.*

Removing the Shell from Memory

▶ **Tip:** *Exit the Shell with Shift-F9 if you plan to come back to it. If you exit by pressing F3 or Alt-F4 or choosing Exit from the File menu, DOS will have to reread your hard disk if you start the Shell again.*

If you want to leave the Shell and take it completely out of memory, too, press F3, or choose Exit from the File menu (its keyboard shortcut is Alt-F4). If you've got other programs running, exit from each of them first, or you'll get a dialog box complaining at you. To exit from a program that you're running, use the method that you normally would in that program.

To get the Shell back after you've removed it from memory, type *dosshell* at the command prompt.

Here's How To...

Get to the command line from the Shell	Choose Command Prompt from the Main group, or press Shift-F9. To get back, type *exit*.
Cancel a command before you've entered it	Press Esc
Repeat a command at the command line	Press F3
Correct a command before you've entered it	Press Backspace and type the correction
Enter a command after you've typed it	Press Enter
Get online help at the command line	Type the command's name followed by /? or *help* followed by the command
Pause a command	Press Ctrl-S or Pause
Stop a command	Press Ctrl-C or Ctrl-Break
Remove the Shell from memory	Choose Exit from the File menu, or press F3 or Alt-F4
Get the Shell back after it's been taken out of memory	Type *dosshell* at the command prompt

Files

4

Rain does not fall on one roof alone.

CAMEROON PROVERB

Everything you store on your computer is stored as a **file.** Your word processing documents are stored as files, and so are your spreadsheets. In fact, your programs themselves are special types of files called executable files, because they run (or "execute").

Creating a File

How do you create a file? Normally, you use a program like WordPerfect or Quattro Pro or PC Paintbrush, although you can create text files (including a special kind of file called a batch file) by using the text editor supplied with DOS 5. (It's appropriately called the Editor, and there's more about using it in the AUTOEXEC.BAT chapter.) When you save the file (store it on disk), you're asked to name it, and that creates the file.

▶ **Tip:** *There's one other way to create a file: by copying it from the keyboard as you type. See COPY in the DOS Commands section if you want to know how to do this.*

Naming Files

DOS makes you follow rigid rules about naming files. You can only use eight characters, so you have to be creative and compress enough information into the name so that you can identify the file again. Here are the characters you can use: all the alphabet (DOS thinks uppercase and lowercase are the same thing), all the numbers, and the characters $ ~ # @ ! ' ( ) { } - _ ^.

▶ **Tip:** *If you use a name that's longer than eight characters, DOS will just chop it off without telling you. MARYLETTER becomes MARYLETT, for example. This can cause a problem if you already have a MARYLETT file.*

Don't ever use these, though:

<> angle brackets

\   backslash

| bar

[] brackets

:   colon

,   comma

= equals

+ plus

"   quotation mark

;   semicolon

/   slash

So you can name a file BOBLETTR or BOB_LTR or BOB, but not BOB LETTER or "BOB's" or BOB*LET.

⚠**Warning:** *Be careful not to name a file with the same name as another file in the same directory. You'll get an "access denied" message if you do.*

Set up a consistent naming system so that you can identify your files weeks and even months after you've saved them. For example, you might want to name a letter you wrote on the second of February as 2_2LET. Or you might want to use the name of the person you wrote the letter to, like SMITHLET. If you're consistent about following a system, you'll stand a better chance of being able to figure out which file is which later.

Extensions

▶ **Tip:** *Extensions are especially important in DOS 5, because they let you associate files with the programs that created them. Once you've associated files with the programs they belong to, you can start the program running and open the file at the same time. You'll see how in the Programs chapter.*

In addition to the eight characters you can use for file names, you'll often see a period and three more characters. This is called an **extension** because it's an addition to the file's basic name. Extensions are used to help identify what kind of file it is. For example, programs always have an extension of .EXE or .COM, like WP.EXE for WordPerfect. Most programs automatically add a special extension to the file name when you save the document or spreadsheet or graphic you're working on, so that it's identified as belonging to that program. WordStar uses .WSD, Lotus 1-2-3 uses .WKS, Excel uses .XLS, and so forth.

In the Shell, program files have icons that are different from document files. Look closely. Program files have a line across the top, while document files look like tiny dog-

eared documents. (You have to be looking at a medium- or low-resolution graphics screen to see this.)

OK, you've named a file. Then you decide that you want to change its name. Maybe somebody gave you the file and you want to rename it to suit your file-naming system. Or maybe you're setting up a new system of file names and want to change a lot of them at the same time. Here's how.

Changing File Names

To rename a file, highlight it and choose Rename from the File menu. You'll see a dialog box asking you to type the new name. After you do that (be sure to follow the rules), choose OK, or just press Enter.

Once you rename a file, it moves to a new alphabetical position in the file list. To see it, just type the first letter of its new name to move to that part of the alphabet.

Renaming a File

▶ **Tip:** *You can also use the DOS REN command (for RENAME) to rename a file.*

You can rename a bunch of files in the Shell at the same time by selecting them and then choosing Rename from the File menu. DOS will give you a dialog box asking for the new name of each one.

Renaming a Bunch of Files

Selecting a single file is easy: just click on it with the mouse or highlight it with the arrow keys. What gets tricky is when you want to select more than one file.

Selecting Files

You can select files that are next to each other by Shift-clicking with the mouse. To Shift-click, click on the first file you want; then hold down the Shift key and click on the last file you want.

With the keyboard, move to the first file you want by using the arrow keys; then press Shift (hold it down) and move to the last file you want.

Selecting Adjacent Files

▶ **Tip:** *Press Home to select the first file in a list or End to select the last one. Type the first letter of a file's name to move to that area of the alphabet.*

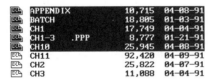

```
APPENDIX        10,715  04-08-91
BATCH           18,805  01-03-91
CH1             17,749  04-04-91
CH1-3    .PPP    8,777  01-21-91
CH10            25,945  04-08-91
CH11            92,420  04-09-91
CH2             25,822  04-07-91
CH3             11,088  04-04-91
```

There are other keyboard shortcuts for selecting without a mouse. (Check out Help.) But it's so much easier with a mouse!

▶ **Tip:** *Pressing Ctrl-/ or choosing Select All from the File menu will select all the files in a list. Ctrl-\ or Deselect All will unselect all but the last file you selected.*

Selecting Nonadjacent Files

▶ **Tip:** *To select files that are in different directories, choose Select Across Directories from the Options menu (press Alt-O and type A to use a keyboard shortcut for this).*

You can even select files that aren't next to each other. To do this, Ctrl-click with the mouse on all the items you want. If you're using the keyboard, first turn on Add mode by pressing Shift-F8. You can then use the arrow keys to move to each item and press the space bar to select it. Press Shift-F8 when all the items are selected.

CH1		17,749	04-04-91
CH1-3	.PPP	8,777	01-21-91
CH10		25,945	04-08-91
CH11		92,420	04-09-91
CH2		25,822	04-07-91
CH3		11,088	04-04-91
CH3	.TWG	6,946	04-08-91

Deselecting Files

Suppose you select a file by mistake? No problem. To deselect one file, press Ctrl and click on it, or, in Add mode, move to it with the arrow keys and use the space bar to deselect it. To deselect all but one file, click on that file. To cancel all selections but the last one, press Ctrl-\ or choose Deselect All.

Deleting Files

⚠ **Warning:** *DOS will display only the file names that are in the current directory, so you won't be able to see all the files you've selected if you've selected across directories. It's easy to delete files by mistake this way.*

Sooner or later, you'll want to delete a file or two. For one thing, you'll eventually run out of room on your disk.

In the Shell, just select the file or files you want to delete and press Del, or choose Delete from the File menu. You'll be prompted about whether you really want to delete the files.

On the command line, you don't get any notice that a file has actually been deleted, but if you try to get a directory listing of it with the DIR command, you'll get the message "file not found." In the Shell, you'll see the file disappear from the screen, if you look closely.

Looking at Different File Views

You can use the View menu to specify whether you want to look at lists of files as well as programs (this is the preset choice, Program/File Lists) or whether you want to view just files, or just programs.

Single File List

If you choose Single File List from the View menu, you'll see just the directory tree and a list of the files in the current directory. As you select each directory in the directory tree window, the file list will change to show the files that are in it.

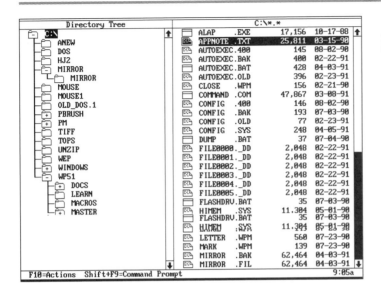

▶ **Tip:** *On your computer, files are organized into a system of directories and subdirectories, like file folders. You'll see more about them in the Directories chapter.*

Single File List

The file's size (in bytes) and the date it was created or most recently changed is shown next to the file's name.

Choosing All Files lets you see all the files on a disk, listed alphabetically, as well as their size, and when they were created or changed. It also shows information about the size of the disk (in bytes), how many files are on it, how much space is available, how many directories are there,

▶ **Tip:** *Using Single File List is like getting a directory listing with the DOS DIR command. You get the same information about the files in the current directory as you do with that command.*

All Files

31

and so forth. As you select each different file, the area on the left changes to show information about the directory the file is in.

If you choose Dual File List, you can see files and directories on two disks, or look at two directories on the same disk. This is handy for when you want to copy or move files from one directory to another.

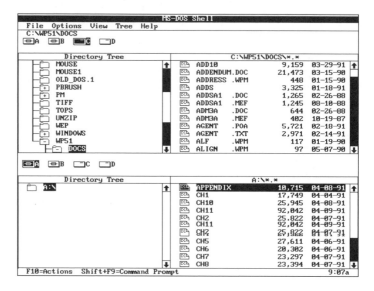

Dual File List

Getting More Information

To get detailed information about a file, select it and choose Show Information from the Options menu. You'll then see an information window about the file showing its name, size, and attributes (more on these soon).

▶ **Tip:** *Choose Show Information to see how much space is left on a disk.*

The Show Information window also tells you the directory's name and size, the size of the disk and number of files on it, the number of directories on the disk, and the space available.

Attributes are special characteristics of a file that you don't normally have to worry about. They indicate to DOS exactly what type of file it is and a few other things about it. Here are the attributes a file can have:

- Hidden—hides the file so that it doesn't appear in a directory listing.

- System—indicates that the file is a DOS system file.

- Archive—indicates whether a file has been used lately.

- Read only—indicates that the file can't be changed.

Most of the time you probably won't need to change a file's attributes, but you can do this quite easily in the Shell (or by using the DOS ATTRIB command). Just select the files whose attributes you want to change (Shift-click for adjacent files, Ctrl-click for files that aren't next to each other) and then select Change Attributes from the File menu. You can then choose whether you want to change the files one at a time or all at once (if you're changing the same attribute on all the files). After that, you can choose which attribute to change and then press Enter. A small symbol next to the attribute indicates that it's on.

Giving a file the read-only attribute is a neat trick for keeping files from being changed by other people (and yourself). If you share a computer with others, you'll appreciate this trick.

You might want to make a file hidden or read only to protect it from getting altered, but the other two attributes are best left to DOS. The archive attribute's important so that DOS can keep track of which files have been backed up, and the system file attribute indicates that a file is part of DOS.

To choose how you want your files displayed, select File Display Options from the Options menu. You can get them sorted in reverse alphabetical order, sort them by size (largest to smallest), sort them by date (most recent first), and so forth.

File Attributes

▶ **Tip:** *Look up ATTRIB in the DOS Commands section to see more details about file attributes.*

▶ **Tip:** *Giving a file the hidden attribute hides it from directory listings so that casual browsers can't see it.*

▶ **Tip:** *Making a file read only doesn't stop people from reading what's in it. It just stops them from changing it or erasing it. It stops you, too, by the way.*

Sorting the File List

▶ **Tip:** *Getting a list that's sorted by date lets you quickly find the files you worked on most recently.*

```
┌─────────────[ File Display Options ]─────────────┐
│ Name:      *.*_                                   │
│                                                   │
│                                   Sort by:        │
│ [ ] Display hidden/system files   ◉ Name          │
│                                   ○ Extension      │
│                                   ○ Date           │
│ [ ] Descending order              ○ Size          │
│                                   ○ DiskOrder      │
│                                                   │
│      ( OK )        ( Cancel )       ( Help )       │
└───────────────────────────────────────────────────┘
```

Seeing What's in a File

To see what's in a file using the Shell, just highlight it and press F9. Neat, huh? Well, it's neat if you can read it. You can't read most files.

A lot of the time what you see will be garbage, though. This is because programs add special formatting characters to their files. If the file is a special kind of file called a **text-only** file (sometimes called an **ASCII file**), you'll be able to read it just fine. If it's a file you've created with a word processing program, you'll be able to read parts of it, but there'll be lots of weird formatting characters.

▶ **Tip:** *On the command line, use the TYPE and MORE commands to see what's in a file.*

Finding Files

Instead of looking through all the different directories and file views to find the file you're looking for, you can use the Shell's Search command to find a file, as long as you know part of its name.

When you choose Search from the File menu, you'll see a dialog box that lets you type the name of the file you're looking for. If you know its name, fine; if you can guess at part of its name, use **wildcards.**

```
┌─────────────[ Search File ]─────────────┐
│ Current Directory is C:\WP51\DOCS        │
│                                          │
│ Search for. .  memo*.*_                  │
│                                          │
│          [X] Search entire disk          │
└──────────────────────────────────────────┘
```

▶ **Tip:** *If you're looking for specific lines in the text of a file, use the FIND command. See the DOS Commands section for details.*

In poker, wild cards match anything. In DOS, they stand for the letters in the name that all the files have in common. In DOS, the ? stands for any one character, and the * stands for any number of characters. So A* means "all files beginning with A (with no extension)" and A*.* means "all files beginning with A and with any extension."

LETTER?.DOC means all files beginning with LETTER and ending in a single character, like LETTER1.DOC, LETTERA.DOC, or LETTER_.DOC.

For example, you may be looking for a file that you know starts with MEMO. Enter MEMO*.* to search for all files beginning with MEMO and ending in anything. Or enter *.EXE to search for all the program (executable) files.

When the search is over, DOS will display all the files that matched the name or the pattern you entered. You can select each one and press F9 to see what's inside it (but this often won't tell you much). Press Esc to get back to the Shell.

> **⚠Warning:** *Although *.* appears in the Search dialog box, don't search for it (*.* means "everything"). That would be meaningless, if you think about it. But this is what DOS will do if you don't enter a file name or a different wildcard pattern.*

> ▶ **Tip:** *Searching the whole disk can take a while, depending on how many files you've got. If you've got a general idea of which directories the file might be in, just search those by unchecking Search Entire Disk, highlighting each directory in turn, and searching it.*

If you didn't really mean to delete a file, you can get it back (if you realize it soon enough). DOS doesn't actually delete a file from the disk; it just marks the space the file takes up as reusable. So if you haven't done a lot of work between the time you deleted the file and the time you realize that you didn't want to do that, you can probably get the file back.

To undelete a file you just deleted, choose Undelete from the Disk Utilities group. You'll get a warning that you might lose the file under some conditions, but if you need it back, what have you got to lose? It's already deleted. Enter the file's name and press Enter.

Instead of using the Disk Utilities group, you can also choose Run from the File menu (or go to the command line) and give the UNDELETE command with the name of the file you deleted by mistake. Remember to click on the drive (or specify it in the command) if the file you're undeleting is on a disk in a different drive.

Undeleting Files

> ▶ **Tip:** *There's a neat trick you can use to make sure you can get your files back. See the AUTOEXEC.BAT chapter and the MIRROR command in the DOS Commands section.*

You'll see the file name with a ? as the first character of its name. Type Y to undelete it. You'll then be asked for the first letter of its name, and if you guess right, DOS will undelete it.

The /LIST that you see in the Undelete dialog box tells DOS to list all the files on the disk that can be undeleted. If you don't remember the exact name of the file you're looking for, press Enter to see this list.

After you've reviewed the file names, choose Undelete again from the Main group and enter the name of the file you want to undelete.

You can use wildcards to undelete groups of files that have similar names. For example, if you deleted a group of files that all ended in .DOC, you could get them back with UNDELETE *.DOC.

What Else Can You Do with Files?

You can copy and move them from one directory to another. See the Directories chapter.

Here's How To...

Create a file	Save it in a program
Name files	Use eight characters plus a three-character extension
Change file names	Select the file and choose Rename from the File menu (or use the DOS REN command)
Select all files	Press Ctrl-/ or choose Select All from the File menu
Select adjacent files	Shift-click, or press Shift and use the arrow keys
Select nonadjacent files	Ctrl-click, or press Shift-F8, (Add mode), use the arrow keys to move to each file, press the space bar to select it, and press Shift-F8 again when you're done

Move files	Drag them, or press F7, or choose Move from the File menu
Copy files	Ctrl-drag them, or press F8, or choose Copy from the File menu (or use the DOS COPY or XCOPY commands)
Deselect all files	Press Ctrl-\ or choose Deselect All from the File menu
Deselect all but one file	Click on it, or, in Add mode, move to it with the arrow keys and press the space bar
Delete files	Select the files and choose Delete from the File menu, or press Del (or use the DOS DEL or ERASE commands)
See just a list of files in the current directory	Choose Single File List from the View menu (or use the DOS DIR command)
Get information about a file	Choose Show Information from the Options menu
Choose how files are displayed	Choose File Display Options from the Options menu
Protect a file from being changed	Select Change Attributes from the File menu and choose the Read Only attribute
See files on two disks, or files in two directories on the same disk	Choose Dual File List from the View menu
See all files on a disk	Choose All Files from the View menu
Use wildcards	The ? represents one character, and the * represents any number of characters or none at all
See what's in a file	Select the file and press F9 (or use the DOS TYPE command)

See just a list of files in the current directory	Choose Single File List from the View menu (or use the DOS DIR command)
Search for a file name	Choose Search from the File by menu and enter the name or the pattern of the name, using wildcards
Select a file	Click on it or use the arrow keys to highlight it
Go to the first or last file in a list	Press Home or End
Go to an area of the alphabet in a list	Type the letter
Undelete a file	Choose Undelete from the Main group and give the name of the file to undelete, or press Enter to see a list of files that can be undeleted (or use the DOS UNDELETE command)

Directories and Subdirectories

> They drew all manner of things—everything that begins with an M... such as mouse-traps, and the moon, and memory, and muchness...
>
> LEWIS CARROLL, *Alice's Adventures in Wonderland*, 1865

On your computer, files are organized into a system of **directories**. Think of a directory as a file folder in a filing cabinet. You can put all kinds of files in a directory—program files, spreadsheets, documents, graphic images, whatever you like. Directories can even hold other directories, called **subdirectories**, just like you stuff folders inside other folders in a filing cabinet. For example, you might have a directory named LOTUS and a subdirectory beneath it named SALES where you kept sales spreadsheets. The entire structure of directories and subdirectories is called the **directory tree,** but it's an upside-down tree with the root on top! Like a lot of things about computers, it's upside down.

▶ **Tip:** *The directory you're in is called the current directory. In the Shell, it's the folder that's highlighted, and you see its name over the disk drive icons at the top. The current drive is the one that's highlighted at the top of the screen.*

The Root Directory

At the top of your directory system is what DOS calls the **root directory.** All the other directories and their subdirectories branch off from it.

When you start the Shell, you always start in the root directory. In the directory tree, it's represented by a folder that has C:\ next to it. The C indicates that you're on drive C, your hard drive.

▶ **Tip:** *The \ is shorthand for the root directory, and that's why you can't use it in a file name.*

▶ **Tip:** *On the command line, you change drives by typing the drive letter, typing a colon (:), and pressing Enter. So if the prompt says A:\>, to change to C:\>, you'd type C: and press Enter. You change directories with the CD command.*

On the command line, when you get that C:\> prompt, or some variation of it, you're at the root directory.

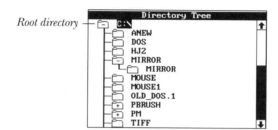

Root directory

Seeing What's in Directories

In the Shell, to see what's in a directory, you can either click on it or use the up and down arrow keys to move through the list of folders. As you move through the folders, the file list on the right changes to show the files that are in them.

Expanding and Collapsing Directories

A tiny + on a folder means that there's at least one subdirectory beneath it. If you click once on the folder with the mouse or highlight it and type a +, the display will change so that you can see these hidden subdirectories, and the + will change to a –. This is called **expanding** a directory, and the opposite—closing everything up again—is called **collapsing** a directory. You can expand all your directories at once, so that you see your entire file structure at a glance (well, everything that will fit in one window), or you can expand just one "branch" of a directory and its related subdirectories.

▶ **Tip:** *At the command line, DIR is the command you use to see what's in directories.*

▶ **Tip:** *You can just type * to expand the selected branch, type + to expand just one level, or press Ctrl-* to expand all of the branches. To collapse a directory, just press –. The gray keys on the numeric keypad (if you have one) are easiest to use.*

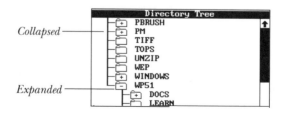

Collapsed

Expanded

To do this, you use the Tree menu. For example, if you wanted to expand one branch, you'd highlight the folder you want to look in and then choose Expand Branch or

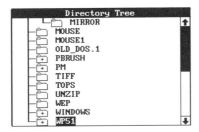

type an asterisk (*). That will expand all the subdirectories under it. To expand *just one level* of subdirectories, choose Expand One Level, or type a +. To expand *all* the folders in the directory tree window, choose Expand All, or press Ctrl-*.

DOS automatically shows you what's on drive C, but you can click on one of the tiny drive icons at the top of the Shell screen to view what's on a floppy disk in one of your floppy disk drives. To use a keyboard shortcut, press Ctrl and type the drive letter. (Your floppy disk drives are always called A and B.) If there's no disk in the drive when you do this, you'll get a "drive not ready" message.

Here's a neat trick. Suppose you want to see what's on the disks in drive A and look in directories on drive C at the same time. Choose Dual File Lists from the View

> **Tip:** *To move directly to a directory when the directory tree window is active, just type the first letter of the directory's name. Pressing Home will select the root directory, and End will select the last directory in a window.*

Looking at What's on Other Drives

> **Tip:** *Pressing Ctrl and typing the drive letter will show you what's on a drive.*

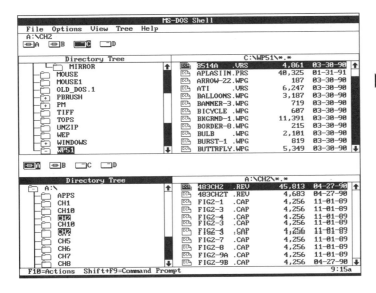

> **Tip:** *To reread what's on a disk (if you've taken one disk out of the drive and put another in, for example) double-click on the drive icon at the top of the screen, or highlight it and press the space bar. Pressing F5 is the keyboard shortcut; it refreshes the screen.*

menu. DOS will then split the screen in two and you can then click on the icon of the disk drive that has the other disk you want to take a look at. You can use this trick to display two directories that are on the same disk, too. Or look at what's on drives A and B.

Whoops! Sometimes DOS may refuse to show you what's on a floppy disk. If you put a blank disk in drive A, you'll get a message saying "General Failure." Don't panic; that just means that the disk hasn't been formatted yet. If you get a message saying that the drive isn't ready, you probably forgot to close the drive door, or you may have put the disk in the drive upside down, or you may have put a high-density disk in a regular disk drive (see the Disks chapter for more about types of disks and drives and how to tell them apart). Take the disk out and look at it. If it's a 5.25-inch disk, you need to put it in with the label face up and the oval cutout going in first. If it's a 3.5-inch disk, the metal shutter has to go in first. And remember to close the 5.25-inch disk drive door.

Looking at All the Files on a Disk Normally the DOS Shell shows you all the directories that are on your hard drive plus any program groups that you've set up (the Programs chapter will tell you how to do

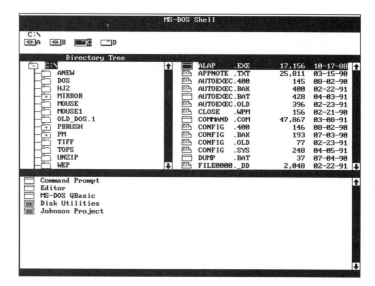

Program/File Lists display

this). This is the Program/File Lists display. You can get a big, full-screen display of everything that's on a disk by selecting the drive and choosing All Files from the View menu. This also gets you a window that has information about the disk, like how many files are on the disk and how much space is left on it.

> ▶ **Tip:** *It's often handy to know how much space is left on a disk if you're trying to figure out whether it can hold more files.*

```
┌─────────────────────── MS-DOS Shell ───────────────────────┐
│ File  Options  View  Tree  Help                            │
│ A:\APPS                                                     │
│ ▢A  ▢B  ▢C  ▢D                                             │
│                          *.*                                │
│                      483APPA .REV    47,563  05-21-90 10:09a│
│  File                483APPAC.REV     6,609  05-21-90 10:32a│
│   Name  : 483APPA.REV 483APPAT.REV   16,429  05-21-90 10:26a│
│   Attr  : ...a       483APPB .REV    12,747  05-10-90 12:26p│
│  Selected    A    C  483APPC .REV     5,943  05-10-90 12:31p│
│   Number:    1    1  483CH1  .REV    37,486  04-27-90  7:34a│
│   Size  :   50,674   483CH2  .REV    45,813  04-27-90  9:00a│
│  Directory           483CH2T .REV     4,683  04-27-90 11:09a│
│   Name  : APPS       483CH3  .REV    58,067  04-27-90 11:41a│
│   Size  :   89,291   483CH4  .REV    57,851  04-27-90  8:42a│
│   Files :        5   483CH5  .REV    32,257  05-08-90 11:35a│
│  Disk                483CH6  .REV    90,666  04-27-90  1:03p│
│   Name  : none       483CH6T .REV     1,000  04-27-90  6:33a│
│   Size  : 1,213,952  483CH7  .REV    95,240  05-13-90  8:25a│
│   Avail :    1,024   483CH8  .REV    84,016  05-14-90 12:15p│
│   Files :      121   483CH8T .REV     2,638  05-13-90  8:26a│
│   Dirs  :       12   483CH9  .REV    62,334  05-14-90 12:45p│
│                      483DISK .REV     2,207  05-13-90  8:20a│
│                      483INTRO.REV    19,434  04-27-90  8:36a│
│                      CH10TOC         20,742  05-05-90 12:19p│
│                      CH5TOC           5,837  05-08-90 11:34a│
│                      CH10TOC         20,742  05-05-90 12:19p│
│                      CH5TOC           5,837  05-08-90 11:34a│
│                      CH8TOC           9,580  05-04-90  2:40p│
│                      CH9TOC           7,151  05-04-90  2:41p│
│                      F1-2    .CAP     4,256  02-20-90  4:26p│
│                      FIG1-2  .CAP     4,256  05-04-99  1:53p│
│ F10=Actions  Shift+F9=Command Prompt              9:16a     │
└─────────────────────────────────────────────────────────────┘
```

> ▶ **Tip:** *You can choose Show Information from the Options menu to get detailed information about a file that you've selected.*

All Files display

Once you've got the All Files display, you'll see the files in the disk, in alphabetical order (names that start with numbers will come first). You can then choose File Display Options from the Options menu and get the files listed by date (most recent first), by size, sorted in reverse order, or listed from largest to smallest, or even sorted into the order that they are on the disk.

> ▶ **Tip:** *If you're looking for a file often, rename it to begin with a number. That way it'll always be at the top of the file list. Don't do this with your program files, though; just your documents.*

So maybe you don't need to see everything that's on a disk, just what's in a directory. The Shell shows files organized by directories when you choose Program/File Lists, Single File List, or Dual File List from the View menu.

If you just want to see the directory tree on the left and a list of what files are in the selected directory, choose Single File List. As you select different directories, the file list will change to reflect what's in them.

Looking at Different Directory Views

▶ **Tip:** *Choose Dual File List if you're copying or moving files from one directory to another. You can see into both directories.*

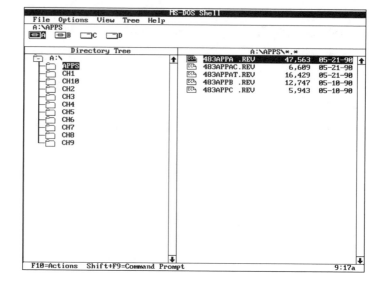

Dual File List display

Looking at Groups of Files

Well, maybe you don't want to look at all of the files in a directory. Directories can get pretty big. You can just look at just the files that have a certain extension or a certain pattern to their names.

▶ **Tip:** *DOS assumes that you always want to see everything, and that's what the *.* at the top of the file list and after Name: in the File Display Options dialog box stands for. This *.* is a wicked little trick. It means "everything."*

The trick here is to again use the File Display Options dialog box. It lets you specify which files you want to look at. You can use the special wildcard characters to stand for the letters in the name that all the files have in common. Remember, the ? stands for any one character, and the * stands for any number of characters. So to see all the files that end in .WPG, you'd enter *.WPG. To see all the files beginning with A and ending with anything, you'd enter A*.*. Or to see all the files that have the pattern MEMO1, MEMO2, MEMO3, and so forth, you'd enter MEMO?.

The notation at the top of the file list is the **path** to the directory you're in—the current directory. The path is the way DOS (and you) can keep track of where things are, if you've got subdirectories within subdirectories. The path is just a list of all the directories that lead to the directory that holds the file you're looking for, just like the house that Jack built.

What's confusing about paths is the cryptic way you have to write them out. You use a backslash to separate each directory name, and you have to remember to put a colon (:) after the drive letter. So C:\WP51\DOCS indicates the DOCS subdirectory of the WP51 directory, which is under the root directory (the first \). And A:\CHAPTERS indicates a directory on the disk in drive A (yes, you can have directories on floppy disks, too).

In the Shell, you don't have to worry too much about paths because you can usually just choose which folder you want to look in, or drag documents to other folders to copy and move them. You may have to type paths sometimes, though—if the directory you're copying a file into isn't visible on the screen, for example, or if you don't have a mouse.

The Path

▶ **Tip:** *In DOS 5, the command line prompt always shows the path to the directory you're in. See PROMPT in the DOS Commands section.*

▶ **Tip:** *When you type a path, remember that the drive is followed by a colon and each directory is separated by a backslash.*

You can create directories of your own and add them to the structure that's already on your hard disk. When you choose Create Directory from the File menu (or press Alt-F and type *e*), you'll see a dialog box listing the directory that's currently highlighted. This is called the **parent directory,** because the new directory you create (the **child**) will be underneath it. If you don't want to create your new directory there, highlight the directory you want the new directory to go under, or highlight the root directory to put the new directory up at the top of your directory tree.

Creating a Directory

▶ **Tip:** *At the command line, you create directories with the MD (Make Directory) command. The XCOPY command will create directories, too. See the DOS Commands section for details.*

▶ **Tip:** *Quickest way to get back to the root directory in the directory tree window: just press Home.*

```
┌─────────────[ Create Directory ]─────────────┐
│                                               │
│   Parent name: C:\WP51                        │
│                                               │
│   New directory name. .  [_              ]    │
│                                               │
│                                               │
│                                               │
│    ┌───────┐    ┌──────────┐    ┌──────┐      │
│    │  OK   │    │  Cancel  │    │ Help │      │
│    └───────┘    └──────────┘    └──────┘      │
└───────────────────────────────────────────────┘
```

When you create a directory, DOS doesn't automatically make it current. Select it to make it current.

Removing a Directory

In the Shell, it's easy. Just highlight the directory you want to delete and press Del. You'll get prompted to make sure that's really what you want to do.

If there's anything in the directory, you'll get an "Access denied" message. Go back and delete any files or subdirectories that are in the directory; you'll be able to delete it then. By the way, at the command line, DEL *.* will delete everything in a directory.

▶ **Tip:** *At the command line, use RD to remove a directory and MD to create one.*

Moving a Directory

To move a directory: first, create the new directory, if it doesn't already exist. Now copy everything in the original directory into the new one. Then delete everything in the original directory; finally, delete the original directory itself. (The XCOPY command can simplify this. See the DOS Commands section.)

Renaming Directories

In the Shell, it's easy: Highlight the directory; then choose Rename and enter the new name. Follow the same rules as file names.. Two subdirectories in the same directory can't have the same name.

At the command line, you'll have to COPY it (or XCOPY it, if it has subdirectories) to a new name, DEL everything in the old directory, and then RD (remove) the old directory.

▶ **Tip:** *You can't rename a directory with the DOS REN command.*

Copying and Moving Files in Directories

You'll often want to reorganize your files into different directories. Before you can copy or move a file, though, you have to select it. The Files chapter has a lot of tips for selecting files, whether they're next to each other or all over the place.

Once you've selected a file (or a group of files), you can use the File menu's Copy and Move commands to put them in other directories, or you can just drag them to their new locations with the mouse, if the destination folder's visible on the screen. Drag to move; Ctrl-Drag to copy.

▶ **Tip:** *Choose Dual File Lists to see into two directories at once.*

If you have a mouse, moving files is really easy in the Shell. Once the file and the directory it's going to be moved into are both visible on the screen, just select the file and drag it into its new directory. If you have Confirm on Mouse Operation checked in the Confirmation options dialog box, you'll be asked to verify that this is what you want to do.

With the keyboard, select the file you want to move and then choose Move from the File menu, or press F7. You'll see the Move dialog box.

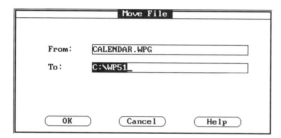

DOS will display the name of the directory that's highlighted. If that's not where you want to move the file, type the path to the directory where you want to move it to and then choose OK.

You can move several files at once if you've selected them first. Choose Select Across Directories from the Options menu to move files from several directories at once. If you're using a mouse, the icons will change to a tiny stack of documents as you drag the last selected file.

Copying files with the mouse is easy, too. Just press Ctrl and drag the file into the folder where you want to copy it.

To copy more than one file, Shift-click to select adjacent files or Ctrl-click to select files that aren't next to each other. If you're copying groups of files by using the keyboard, press Shift-F8 to turn on Add mode and use the space bar to select the ones you want. Remember to turn on Select Across Directories on the Options menu if you want to copy files that are in more than one directory.

The advantage to using the Copy command (or F8) instead of dragging file icons is that you can use wildcards to speed up the copying process if you're copying files that

Moving Files

▶ **Tip:** *Alt-drag to move; Ctrl-drag to copy.*

▶ **Tip:** *To move files using the command line, you have to copy them into their new locations and then delete them.*

⚠**Warning:** *If you turned on Select Across Directories and forgot that it was on, you may find that you've got a whole bunch of files selected when you go to copy or move. Press Ctrl-\ to deselect all of them; then go back and select the one you want to work with. And turn off that pesky Select Across Directories unless you really want to do that.*

Copying Files

▶ **Tip:** *The keyboard shortcut for Copy is F8 and for Move is F7.*

▶ **Tip:** *Keep Confirm on Replace checked in the Confirmation options box so that you don't copy one file over another one that has the same name.*

have similar names. Suppose you want to copy everything ending in .WKS. You can just put *.WKS in the Copy dialog box. To copy every file beginning with A in the current directory, you'd enter A*.* To copy both the files named BROWN.TXT and BRAUN.TXT, you could enter BR??N.TXT.

Copying a File and Renaming It, Too

▶ **Tip:** *This is how to make a copy of a file in the same directory.*

If you want your new copy to have a different name, use the keyboard to copy it. Then just enter its new name at the end of the path. For example, if you wanted to copy the file 3270.TXT into the directory C:\WINDOWS but name the copy NEW.TXT, you'd enter it like this:

```
┌─────────────────────────────────────────────────┐
│                    ▐ Copy File ▌                  │
│                                                   │
│                                                   │
│     From:    ┌3270.TXT──────────────────────┐     │
│     To:      │c:\windows\new.txt            │     │
│              └──────────────────────────────┘     │
│                                                   │
│                                                   │
└─────────────────────────────────────────────────┘
```

Copying Directories

Here's a tip for copying entire directories in the Shell. To copy all the files in one directory into another directory, choose the directory you want to copy. Then choose Select All from the File menu (or press Ctrl-/). Choose Copy; then type the path to the directory where you want to copy all the files and press Enter (or click OK). If the directory doesn't exist, you'll need to create it first.

Plan Ahead

Whatever filing system you use, be sure to allow for future expansion. Files, like coat hangers, have a way of multiplying when you're not looking. If you have a directory structure with too many subdirectory levels, it'll soon get awkward to move between them, because there'll be so many different levels. Three subdirectories under a directory is about the limit. Beyond that, it starts getting irritating to move through a bunch of subdirectories to find the files you want to work with.

Select a directory	Up and down arrow
Select the root directory	Home
Select the last directory	End

Expand a selected directory one level	+
Expand a branch	*
Expand all	Ctrl-*
Collapse a directory	–

Keyboard Shortcuts for Expanding and Collapsing Directories

Change the current directory and see what's in it	Click on it or move to it with the arrow keys (or use the DOS CD and DIR commands)
See directories on another drive	Select its disk drive icon or press Ctrl and type the drive letter (or use the DIR command and specify a drive)
Reread a disk	Double-click on the drive icon
See into two directories at once	Choose Dual File Lists from the View menu
Sort a directory listing	Choose File Display Options from the Options menu
Look at groups of files with similar names in a directory	Choose File Display Options and enter a wildcard pattern
Create a directory	Choose Create Directory from the File menu (or use the DOS MD command)

Here's How To...

Go to the root directory in the directory tree window	Press Home
Remove a directory	Select it and press Del (or use the DOS RD command). It has to be empty first.
Move a directory	Select everything in it and copy it into another directory; delete everything in it; then remove the original directory
Move files	Select them and drag them, or press F7, or choose Move from the File menu
Copy files	Select them and Ctrl-drag them, or press F8, or choose Copy from the File menu (or use the DOS COPY or XCOPY commands)
Copy a file and rename it	Press F8 and enter the new name at the end of the path
Copy directories	Select all the files in it and press F8; then type the path to the new directory

Disks

6

> Memory is the thing you forget with.
>
> ALEXANDER CHASE, *Perspectives*, 1966

Everything you do with your computer is either stored on floppy or hard disks or in ROM or put into your computer via a floppy disk (unless you're on a network or using a modem). So disks are very important. If you don't treat them right, your computer won't work right.

If you're using 5.25-inch disks, take one out and look at it. It has a right side and a wrong side. The right side is the smooth one, and the wrong side has seams. You always want to put disks into your disk drive with the right side up and the oval cutout going into the drive first, pointing away from you. And remember to close the drive door when the disk is all the way in.

On one side of the disk there'll usually be a little square cutout. This is called the **write-protect notch** because when it's covered over, whatever's on the disk can't be changed, or written on. There may be a tab over the notch that you can remove. Once the tab's removed, you can change whatever's on the disk. If there isn't any notch, that disk is permanently write-protected.

Big Floppy Disks

▶ **Tip:** *It's a good idea to keep your program disks— those that you buy— write-protected so that you don't ever change what's on any of them.*

Little Floppy Disks

If you're using 3.5-inch disks, they look a lot different from the 5.25-inch kind. The right side on them just shows a rectangular metal shutter. The wrong side has a round metallic insert in the middle. You put this kind of disk into the drive with the metal shutter going in first and the right side up. The drive door for this kind of disk will automatically close when the disk is in far enough.

On the top (right) side of the disk there'll be a square hole. This is the **write-protect tab.** If it's closed, you can change whatever's on the disk. If it's open, you can't. There's a slider on the back of the disk that lets you open and close this tab. Isn't it annoying that the computer world is so inconsistent? This is just the opposite of the way write protection works on the 5.25-inch floppy disks.

Labels

Make labels for your floppy disks so that you can tell what's on them. Use a felt-tip pen, because pressing down with a pencil or a ballpoint pen can damage the delicate surface of the disk. Don't cover the notch (on 5.25-inch disks) with the label if you want to be able to change what's on the disk. Don't cover the oval cutout or the metal shutter (on 3.5-inch disks) with the label. Don't touch the part of the disk that you can see in the oval or round cutouts.

Disk Capacities

▶ **Tip:** *The high-density 3.5-inch disks have two square holes! That's how you can tell them from the 720K disks. Unfortunately, there's no such trick for telling unlabeled 5.25-inch disks apart by just glancing at them.*

You'll hear disks talked about in terms of their capacity. "Is that a 360K disk, or is it 1.2 meg?" As you saw in Chapter 1, K stands for kilobyte, which is 1024 bytes. Meg is short for megabyte (Mb), which is a thousand kilobytes (a little over a million bytes). Here's a table that will take some of the mystery out of the jargon:

Size	Capacity	In bytes, that's	Also called
5.25	360K	368,640	Double density
5.25	1.2 Mb	1,228,800	High density
3.5	720K	737,280	Double density
3.5	1.44 Mb	1,474,560	High density

Which kind of disk should you use? Well, you can't use the high-density disks unless you have a high-density disk drive, and you can't use the 3.5-inch disks unless you have a 3.5-inch disk drive, so that narrows your choices.

If you have a high-density disk drive, use high-density disks for your backups: they're more expensive, but you can put lots more files on them and keep the number of floppy disks you have to store to a minimum. If you're planning to swap disks with other people, who may not be so lucky as to have a high-density drive, though, better use the 360K disks, which almost everybody can accept (except those of you with PS/2s or laptops).

▶ **Tip:** *A disk's sleeve is a paper cover that you store the disk in to keep dust out of it. When you read "take the disk out of its sleeve," that's referring to this paper envelope, not to the plastic cover that the disk is sealed in! The smaller 3.5-inch disks don't have sleeves because the shutter automatically closes to keep out dust.*

Formatting Disks

Before you can use a disk, DOS has to prepare it so that it can read it. This is called **formatting** (on a Mac, it's called initializing. Same thing).

Usually, when you buy a box of disks, they're not formatted. (You can buy preformatted disks, but they're sort of expensive.) But there'll probably be times when you're looking at a blank, unlabeled disk, wondering whether it's ready to use or not. How can you tell whether a disk needs to be formatted? Easy. Put it in the drive and try to get a directory listing of what's on it. (In the Shell, click on the drive icon, or highlight it and press Enter.) If you get the sort of scary message "General failure," don't panic. It just means that the disk in drive A hasn't been formatted yet, not that your computer has generally failed. Choose Cancel to cancel the command; then go ahead and format the disk.

If you get a list of files that are on the disk, it's already been formatted. If there's any space available on it, you can use it for storing more files. To see how much space is available, highlight the disk drive icon, choose Show Information from the Options menu, and check out what's next to "Avail." If you're running the

▶ **Tip:** *When you format a disk, everything that's on it is wiped out. With DOS 5, you can get it back, though, with the UNFORMAT and REBUILD commands. They're discussed in the DOS Commands section of this book.*

```
┌──── Show Information ────┐
│ File                     │
│   Name  : 483CH2.REV     │
│   Attr  : ...a           │
│ Selected     A     C     │
│   Number:    1     1     │
│   Size  :       73,508   │
│ Directory                │
│   Name  : CH2            │
│   Size  :       88,800   │
│   Files :           11   │
│ Disk                     │
│   Name  : none           │
│   Size  :    1,213,952   │
│   Avail :        1,024   │
│   Files :          121   │
│   Dirs  :           12   │
│  ( Close )     ( Help )  │
└──────────────────────────┘
```

DIR command, you'll see a number of "bytes free" at the bottom of the listing. You can delete files you don't want to free more space.

Formatting a Floppy Disk

OK, you've got a brand-new floppy disk. Here's how to format it in the Shell:

1. Choose Format from the Disk Utilities menu (you can double-click on the Disk Utilities icon if you have a mouse). You'll see a dialog box asking you for parameters. If you want to format the disk as a system disk, or format it in a different capacity, you'd enter some cryptic options here (they'll be discussed later in this chapter).

2. Just press Enter to format what's in drive A. If you want to format a disk in drive B, type *b:* and press Enter.

3. You'll be prompted to insert the disk and press Enter. When you do, DOS will go ahead and format it. It'll tell you what capacity it's formatting the disk in and how it's doing.

> **Tip:** *Check to see that nothing's on a disk (or that there's nothing there that you want to keep) before you format it. To do this in the Shell, click on the icon of the disk drive, or highlight it and press Enter. With the command line, get a directory listing with the DIR command.*

```
┌───────────────────────── Format ─────────────────────────┐
│                                                           │
│   Enter the drive to format.                              │
│                                                           │
│   Parameters  . . .  [a:_                             ]   │
│      ( OK )            ( Cancel )          ( Help )        │
└───────────────────────────────────────────────────────────┘
```

> ⚠ **Warning:** *Don't try to format regular-density disks in a high-density disk drive without using some special options at the end of the command. See "Formatting Disks in Different Capacities" later in this chapter.*

When it's done, it'll ask you if you want to format another disk. Type either Y or N and press Enter. If it's N, press any key to get back to the Shell, if you started out from there.

Quick Formatting

> **Tip:** *Use Quick Format on used disks.*

If a disk has already been formatted and has files on it, you can do a quick format on it in the Shell. Choose Quick Format from the Disk Utilities menu instead of Format. This will clean off everything on the disk very quickly. It's a lot faster than doing a regular format.

Instead of using the Disk Utilities menu, you can also use the FORMAT command by running it from the File menu or the command line. Enter the command like this: FORMAT A: or FORMAT B: and press Enter. Be sure to tell DOS which drive the disk is in, or it'll tell you that you have to specify a drive letter.

When the formatting's done, you'll be asked if you want to give the disk a label.

⚠Warning: *Don't format C: or D: unless you're really formatting your hard disk! DOS will warn you if you try to do this.*

Using a Label

You can give disks an electronic label of as many as 11 characters. You can use spaces here, so your disk labels can be more meaningful than file names! It's OK not to give a newly formatted disk a label. But you may want to label them to identify their owner (you) or to indicate what kinds of files are stored on the disk, like OCT REPORTS. It's up to you.

Doing the Job

Formatting disks is a dull, time-consuming job. You should probably put on some of your favorite music and sit there and format as many disks as you can stand, just so you'll have a good supply handy. Formatting disks gets rather mechanical after a while.

Put a (real) label on the disks that have been formatted so that you don't waste time formatting them again! I put a blank label on the ones I've formatted. If they already have labels, you can put a tiny check in the corner, just something that tells you "I've been formatted."

Formatting Disks in Different Capacities

DOS knows what kind of disk drives you have, and it will format the disks you put in them accordingly. However, you may sometimes want to format a 360K disk in a high-density (1.2 Mb) disk drive, so that you can exchange it with other folks who may not have a high-density drive. You can do that by giving the FORMAT command as *format a: /f:360.* (You can either use the Disk Utilities' Format command or run the FORMAT command at the command line.)

You can also format 720K disks in 1.44 Mb (3.5-inch) drives. To do that, give the FORMAT command as *format b: /f:720.* (Use the letter of the drive you're using.)

⚠Warning: *Don't try to format a 360K or 720K disk as a high-density disk. And don't try to format a high-density disk as a lower-density disk. It may look like the formatting has been done, but you'll find later that it may cause problems.*

Formatting a System Disk

▶ **Tip:** *You can use the Uninstall disk you created when you installed DOS 5 as an emergency startup disk.*

▶ **Tip:** *If you're using a disk that's already been formatted, you can just run the SYS command to put the system files on it. SYS B:. for example, puts the system files on a formatted disk in drive B. With DOS 5, you don't have to remember to also copy the file COMMAND.COM onto the disk, like you did with earlier versions of DOS; DOS does it for you.*

You can also format a disk with the DOS system files on it so that you can use it to start your computer, if you have to, without using your hard disk. Normally, you don't need to put the system files on disks you format, because you just use them for storing data, not starting your computer. If you put a disk that has system files in drive A and restart the computer, DOS will start from it, bypassing your hard disk.

Once your computer has started again, you can use this disk, if you have to, to reformat your hard disk and restore your backed-up files onto it.

```
┌─────────────────────────────────────────────┐
│                    Run                       │
│                                              │
│  Command Line . .  format a: /s_            │
│                                              │
│        ( OK )          ( Cancel )           │
└─────────────────────────────────────────────┘
```

To format a disk with the DOS system files on it, just give an extra /S option to the FORMAT command. For a disk in drive A, you'd use FORMAT A: /S, for example.

Once you've got the system files and COMMAND.COM on the disk, that's really all you need to run DOS from that floppy disk. It's a good idea, though, to also copy from your DOS directory CHKDSK.EXE (so that you can check the hard disk), FORMAT.COM (in case you have to reformat the hard disk), and BACKUP.EXE and RESTORE.EXE (in case you can salvage some files from the hard disk). Label the disk "emergency disk" and keep it in a safe place. Then, if your hard disk fails, and your Uninstall disk isn't to be found, you can restart your computer with this disk in drive A.

After your computer's restarted, you can use one of the special utility programs like the Norton Utilities, if you have it, to see what happened to your hard disk and perhaps repair it.

For example, at the A> prompt, you can use the CHKDSK command to inspect your hard disk (the kind of information this command gives is explained in the DOS commands section). If you get a message that there are an enormous number of bad sectors, you can reformat it.

Let's all hope that you never have to do this, because formatting wipes out everything on your hard disk, but the day may come. You may start to get serious error messages about your hard disk, or you may have bought a new hard disk that hasn't been formatted yet.

If you have to format a hard disk that's not working right, here's how to do it. First, turn your computer off, put a DOS disk (either the Uninstall disk or the disk labeled "emergency" that you made) in drive A, and turn it on again. Tell DOS the date and time if it asks.

You'll see an A:\> prompt, because the computer has started from drive A instead of drive C this time. At the prompt, type *format c: /s* and press Enter. (This will put the system files on your hard disk.) You'll then be prompted about whether this is really what you want to do. After the formatting is done, you'll be asked for a volume label. You can give your hard disk a name of up to 11 characters, including spaces. You might want to call it "Drive C," or use your name or, after what you've been through, name it "Titanic." Or use no label at all.

If you get error messages when you try to format the disk, there's probably more wrong with it than you want to deal with. Call your dealer or a guru.

If you're formatting a brand-new hard disk right out of the box, there are a couple of other things you may need to do. First, you need to check if low-level formatting has been done on the disk (they usually come with this done to them, or it may be done automatically the first time you start the computer. If not, check to see if any additional instructions came with the disk, and follow them. Then you can run the Setup program to install DOS 5 (see the appendix) and it will format your hard disk.

Formatting a Hard Disk

▶ **Tip:** *Don't do this unless you have to! If you have to, you'll know. Nothing will be working right.*

Here's How To...

Protect a 5.25" disk	Cover the write-protect notch
Protect a 3.5" disk	Uncover the write-protect notch
Format a disk	Choose Format from the Disk Utilities group, or use the DOS FORMAT command
See how much space is available on a disk	Choose Show Information from the Options menu, or use the DIR or CHKDSK commands
Do a quick format on a used disk to free space on it	Choose Quick Format from the Disk Utilities group or use the FORMAT /Q command
Format a 360K 5.25" disk in a high-density drive	Give the options as A: /F:360 (use the letter of your drive)
Format a 720K 3.5" disk in a high-density drive	Give the options as B: /F:720 (use the letter of your drive)
Make a startup disk	Use the /S parameter with the Format command on a disk that's being formatted, or use the DOS SYS command on a disk that's already formatted

Programs

Put all your eggs in one basket and—watch that basket.

MARK TWAIN, *Pudd'nhead Wilson's Calendar*, 1894

One of the hottest new features of DOS 5 is that it lets you have several programs in memory at once and switch between them almost instantly. You can be running a word processing program and switch over to your spreadsheet to check a few facts and dates, or you can look up someone's name and address in your database quickly. How many programs you can run depends on how much memory you have, but I've run WordPerfect and Lotus 1-2-3 at the same time on a plain old IBM XT with no problem at all.

When you first start DOS 5, the Shell screen shows only the Main group of programs—Command Prompt, Editor, QBasic, and the Disk Utilities. You can add programs to this group and create new groups of your own. This chapter will show you how to do that, and it will also show you some new ways to start programs.

Running Programs

You can run programs in several different ways with DOS 5:

- By choosing Run from the File menu and entering the command used to start the program

- By going out to the DOS command prompt (press Shift-F9 or choose Command Prompt from the Main group) and starting the program as you normally would

- By selecting a program from the file list (you can just double-click on it with a mouse)

- By selecting a program item from a program group (double-click on it, too)

- By selecting a program file or a document that's been "associated" with a program (you'll see how to do that in this chapter).

Using the Run Command

▶ **Tip:** *This is a good way to run programs you don't use often.*

The File menu's Run command lets you start a program from within the Shell. Just enter the command you use to start the program in the Run dialog box. For example, to run Microsoft Word, you'd just enter *word* in the Run dialog box and choose OK.

```
┌─────────────────────────────Run─────────────────────────┐
│                                                          │
│  Command Line . .   word_                                │
│                     ┌──────────────────────────────────┐ │
│                     └──────────────────────────────────┘ │
│                                                          │
│         (     OK     )        (    Cancel    )           │
└──────────────────────────────────────────────────────────┘
```

▶ **Tip:** *See the AUTOEXEC.BAT chapter for how to put a program in your path so that you don't have to change directories to run it.*

If you normally have to change to a specific directory to start the program, you'll need to enter the path to it. If you always had to change to the WORD directory to run Word, you'd enter C:\WORD\WORD, for example.

You can also run DOS commands by entering them in the Run dialog box. When you install DOS, the Setup program puts in your AUTOEXEC.BAT file the path to where these commands are stored. This is usually a directory called C:\DOS. So you could just enter *format a:* to format a disk in Drive A, for example.

Using the DOS Command Prompt

You can also use the DOS command prompt to start programs. If you've used DOS before, this is the way you've always started them.

To use the DOS command prompt, choose it from the Main group, or press Shift-F9. When you're done with the command line, you can get back to the Shell by typing *exit*. To remove the Shell from memory, choose Exit from the File menu or press F3 or Alt-F4.

You can start a program running just by choosing its name in the file list. Double-click on it with the mouse, or move the highlight to it with the arrow keys and press Enter. Programs always have an .EXE or .COM extension, and their icons are different from document icons (documents are dog-eared, with one corner turned down).

You can start a program that's in a program group just by double-clicking on its name (or highlighting its name and pressing Enter, if you haven't got a mouse). For example, to use the Backup program in the Disk Utilities group, open the group and choose Backup Fixed Disk.

If a document's been associated with a program, you can choose its name to open it and start the program running. You'll see how to associate documents and programs later in this chapter.

Starting a Program by Choosing Its Name

```
  CONFIG   .SYS
  DUMP     .BAT
```

If you're running a special kind of program called a **pop-up program,** (also sometimes called a TSR), you may need to repaint the screen after you've quit the program, because it may still be visible. Repaint Screen is on the View menu, and its shortcut is Shift-F5.

Sometimes you may need to refresh the screen display, too. For example, if you've created new files or deleted old ones in a word processing program, the screen may not reflect the changes. Pressing F5 will update the screen, or you can choose Refresh from the View menu. When you refresh the screen, your hard disk is read all over again and you go back to the root directory. Very annoying.

Refreshing and Repainting the Screen

The Task Swapper is the neat feature that lets you switch between programs that you've started running. To use it, choose Enable Task Swapper from the Options menu. You'll see a small black symbol next to Task Swapper when it's on.

Then start the programs you want to switch among. In the file list or program list, double-click on the program you want to add or highlight it and press Shift-Enter. As soon as the program starts, press Ctrl-Esc to get back to the Shell. Then start the next program you want to be able to switch to. After you start each one, it'll be listed in a new area of the Shell screen called the active task list.

Using the Task Swapper

▶ **Tip:** *To cycle between all the programs you've got running, hold down Alt and press Tab again and again. To return to the Shell, press Ctrl-Esc.*

```
┌─────────────────────────────────────────┐
│            Active Task List              │
├─────────────────────────────────────────┤
│ WP.EXE                                   │
│ MIRROR.EXE                               │
└─────────────────────────────────────────┘
```

Once the programs are listed in the active task list, you can double-click on it to switch to it or move to it with the arrow keys and press Enter, if you don't have a mouse.

While you're in a program and you've got several running, you can hold down the Alt key and press Tab to see the name of the next program in the active task list. Release Alt when you see the name of the one you want to switch to.

▶ **Tip:** *Sometimes you may be asked to press Ctrl-C to exit from a special kind of program called a pop-up program. Then just press any key to get back to the Shell.*

When you exit from the program, its name is removed from the active task list. You'll need to exit from all the programs you have running before you can exit from the Shell, or you'll get and rebuked with a dialog box.

If a program hangs up on you, go to the Shell (press Ctrl-Esc) highlight its name in the active task list, and delete it. To be on the safe side, restart your computer, just in case there might be problems with the unexpected exit.

Returning to the Shell from Windows

Windows runs beautifully under DOS 5; it's thankful for all that extra memory. But you can't return to the Shell with Ctrl-Esc from Windows, because that key combination brings up the Task List in Windows. To return to the Shell from Windows, exit from Windows and then press any key.

Setting Up Program Groups

▶ **Tip:** *Just because you put a program or a document into a group doesn't mean that you have to always start it from the group. You can still start it just as you've always done.*

You can set up groups of your own so that they'll appear in the program list in the Shell. For example, you might like to organize your work by project or by client and keep all the programs and documents you work with every day in each group. Or if you work with several graphics programs, you might put them all in one group so that you can find them easily. You can have a copy of a program in as many groups as you like; putting a program in a group just gives you a new way to start it. It doesn't really make another copy of it that eats up room on your hard disk.

To use an item in a group, double-click on the group's name to open the group (or use the arrow keys and Enter). You can then choose an item from that group. To close a program group, do the same thing.

To create a group of your own, first display the group you want to add the new group to. For instance, if it's to go in the Main group, display the Main group. (Have the highlight on Command Prompt, Editor, or MS-DOS Qbasic.) Then choose New from the File menu. You'll see a dialog box; select Program Group and then OK.

Creating a Group

▶ **Tip:** *You need to be looking at the Program/ File List or the Program List view to create a new group.*

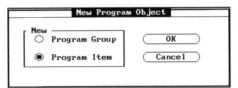

You'll then see the Add Group dialog box. In this one, type the name you want your new group to have. You can use spaces and as many as 23 characters. Press Tab to move to the next line.

▶ **Tip:** *You can also add a Help message (up to 255 characters) about what the group is for. If you're setting up groups for others, this might be a good idea.*

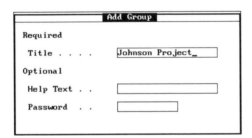

You can also assign a password to your new group. If you're sharing a computer with others, this is a way of getting privacy: no one can open your group except those who know the password. (Anybody can run a program from the DOS prompt, though.)

When you've set your group up, choose OK. You'll see the group's name and an icon for it (if you're using a graphics display) appear in the program list.

▶ **Tip:** *Better write that password down in a secret place somewhere because "paper remembers so that you can forget."*

If you decide later that you want to change the group name, choose Properties from the File menu. You can change the name, the password, and the Help message, if there's one. (You have to know the original password, though.)

Adding Items

▶ **Tip:** *Make sure the name of the group you want to add the item to is at the top of the program list.*

Now you've got a new, empty group, so the next step is to add items to it. They can be either programs or documents. Say you want to add WordPerfect to a group. Highlight the group name and open it. Then choose New from the File menu. This time, click Program Item if it's not already selected.

```
╔══════════════ Add Program ══════════════╗
║                                          ║
║  Program Title . . . .  ┌WordPerfect───┐ ║
║                         └──────────────┘ ║
║  Commands  . . . . . .  ┌wp────────────┐ ║
║                         └──────────────┘ ║
║  Startup Directory . .  ┌──────────────┐ ║
║                         └──────────────┘ ║
║  Application Shortcut Key    ┌ALT+W────┐ ║
║                              └─────────┘ ║
║  [X] Pause after exit    Password . . ┌──┐║
║   ┌────┐  ┌──────┐  ┌────┐  ┌─────────┐ ║
║   │ OK │  │Cancel│  │Help│  │Advanced.│ ║
║   └────┘  └──────┘  └────┘  └─────────┘ ║
╚══════════════════════════════════════════╝
```

Type the name that you want to appear in the group in the Program Title box. It doesn't have to be the real name of the program; you can use something more descriptive. In the Commands box, type the *exact command* you use to start the program. If you normally start WordPerfect with the WP command, type *wp*.

If you want to change to a different directory when you start the program, type the path to that directory in the Startup Directory box. Suppose, for example, that you keep Microsoft Word in a directory named C:\WORD but you want to make the C:\WORD\DOCS directory current when you start Word so that you save all your documents there. In this case you'd type C:\WORD\DOCS in the Startup Directory box.

If you want to be able to switch to the program with a special shortcut key sequence, use the Application Shortcut Key box. Once you've assigned a shortcut key, pressing that key sequence switches you to the program directory once it's running and displayed in the active task list. You won't have to press Alt-Tab to cycle through your running programs or choose the program's name from the active task list.

The shortcut key you select has to be either a Shift, Alt, or Ctrl key combination. If a combination's already been used, DOS won't let you have it as a shortcut key. For example, Alt-F opens the File menu, so you can't use that. You might want to choose Ctrl-W for WordPerfect, just something that's easy to remember.

> **Tip:** *Check out Help to see a list of combinations that are already taken.*

Keep Pause After Exit checked if you want to be able to return to the Shell when you exit from the program.

You can also enter a password. If you do, you'll be prompted for it before DOS will start the program.

When you're done, choose OK.

Now here's a neat trick. You can add documents to program groups, too. The trick is to give the document's name as the "Program Title" (you can use a description here, too) and then enter the path to the document in the Commands box, putting the command used to start the program first. If you forget the program command, the document won't open.

> **Tip:** *You can add documents to your groups, too.*

```
╔════════════════ Add Program ════════════════╗
║                                              ║
║  Program Title . . . .  ┌Floor Plan───────┐  ║
║                         └─────────────────┘  ║
║  Commands  . . . . . .  ┌wp c:\wp51\ch2_───┐ ║
║                         └─────────────────┘  ║
║  Startup Directory . .  ┌─────────────────┐  ║
║                         └─────────────────┘  ║
║  Application Shortcut Key  ┌──────────────┐  ║
║                           └──────────────┘   ║
║  [X] Pause after exit    Password . . ┌────┐ ║
║                                       └────┘  ║
║   ( OK )   ( Cancel )   ( Help )  ( Advanced... ) ║
╚══════════════════════════════════════════════╝
```

Here WordPerfect will open the document named CH2 when you click on Floor Plan.

> **Tip:** *Main's always listed so that you can get back to it.*

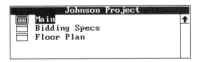

Copying Program Items

▶ **Tip:** *Use the Reorder command to reorder the items in a group and put the ones you use most often at the top. Select the item; choose Reorder; then select the new location and press Enter or double-click.*

A quick way to get programs and documents into the groups you create is to copy them from groups that you've already set up. To do this, just open the group that already has the program in it; then select the program you want to copy. Then choose Copy from the File menu and open the group you want to copy the program into. To complete the copy, press F2. Unfortunately, you can't drag with the mouse or use the F8 keyboard shortcut to copy program items.

Remember, you can have several copies of a program or document in different groups. Choosing Copy doesn't really create a new copy of the program on your hard disk; it just gives you a new way to run it.

Deleting Programs and Groups

▶ **Tip:** *This doesn't delete the program from your hard disk,.*

You can delete a program from a group by highlighting it and pressing Del. If a password's been assigned, you'll need to know it to delete the program.

To delete a group, delete all the items in it first; then delete the group.

Associating Files

⚠**Warning:** *If you've chosen Select Across Directories, you may not see the extension you want in the Associate dialog box. Go back and Deselect All (Ctrl-\).*

One other neat thing you can do with DOS 5 is to associate documents with the programs that "own" them. After a document's been associated with a program, double-clicking on its name or choosing it with the keyboard starts the program and opens the document at the same time.

When you associate documents, you tell DOS that all the files ending in a certain extension are associated with a certain program.

For example, to associate all the files that end in .IGF with the program HiJaak, you'd highlight one of the .IGF files and then choose Associate from the File menu. When the dialog box comes up, fill it out with the command used to start the program, in this case hj.exe.

```
┌──────────────────[ Associate File ]──────────────────┐
│                                                        │
│   '.IGF' files are associated with:                    │
│                                                        │
│   hj.exe_                                              │
│                                                        │
│                                                        │
│                                                        │
│                                                        │
│      (  OK  )        ( Cancel )        ( Help )         │
└────────────────────────────────────────────────────────┘
```

An alternate way to do it is to highlight the program, choose Associate, and in the dialog box type in all the different extensions you want to associate with it, separating each one with a space. This is a faster way if you're associating more than one extension with a program.

The very first time you start the Shell, you see the Program/File Lists. You can choose Program List to see just program groups and the active task list. If you've running a lot of programs at once, this may be the view you'd like to see instead if all the files and directories.

Viewing Program Groups

▶ **Tip:** *DOS remembers what view you looked at last and shows that view to you the next time you start your computer.*

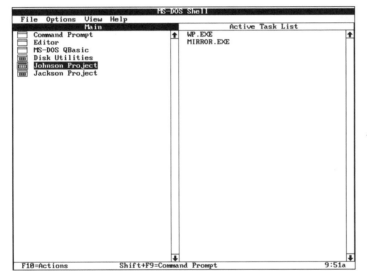

Program List

Here's How To...

Run a program	Choose Run from the File menu or go to the DOS prompt and enter the command you normally use; select the program from the file list; or select a document that's associated with a program; or select the program from a group
Use the DOS prompt	Press Shift-F9 or choose Command Prompt from the Main group
Exit to DOS	Press F3 or Alt-F4 or choose Exit from the File menu
Run several programs	Choose Enable Task Swapper from the Options menu; start the programs
Cycle among programs	Press Alt-Tab or choose a program's name from the active task list
Switch from a program to the active task list	Press Ctrl-Esc
Create a group	Open the group you want to add the new group to (usually Main); choose New from the File menu; select Program Group
Change a group's name, password, or Help screen	Highlight the group; choose Properties from the File menu
Open a program group	Highlight it and press Enter or double-click on it
Add a program to a group	Highlight the group; choose New from the File menu; select Program Item

Add a document to a group	Same as adding a program, but fill out the Command box with the command used to start the program, followed by the path to the document
Copy a program item into a group	Select the program you want to copy; choose Copy from the File menu; open the group you want to copy the program into; press F2
Delete a program item from a group	Highlight the item's name in the group; press Del
Delete a group	Delete all the program items in it first
Associate files and programs	Highlight a file that has the extension you want to associate or highlight the program; choose Associate from the File menu
View just programs	Choose Program List from the View menu

Backups

A good scare is worth more than good advice.

EDGAR WATSON HOWE, *Country Town Sayings*, 1911

Sooner or later, something will go wrong with your computer or your disks. Not "may," *will*. Also, there's the possibility of human error: you may accidentally erase a directory full of files you wanted to keep and not find out until several days later that that's what you did. To protect your work, you need to make backups—copies of all the work you do and all the programs you've bought.

That doesn't mean that you have to use the BACKUP command or purchase a fancy backup utility program, though. You can just make disk copies of all your program disks and copies of all your important documents; this is what I do. But depending on how you work, you may want to back up your entire hard disk every so often to keep everything up to date.

No matter how careful you are, something can happen. This happened to me. I was working in WordPerfect when everything went wrong and I found myself out in DOS again. I called WordPerfect Corporation, thinking it was the program that was at fault, and we had a long conversation about what I was doing (running a macro) and what had happened. They said (I've boiled the conversation down to its essence), "Cosmic ray." I called a fellow who was a DOS expert and told him what was going on and he said, "Cosmic ray." (Actually, he said my FAT was broken—I thought that sounded like a good thing at first—but he meant my file

▶ **Tip:** *If you're a person who needs to back up your whole hard disk periodically, think about buying a second hard disk or a tape drive for backups so that you don't have to wrestle with a million floppies!*

allocation table, which DOS uses to keep track of where everything is.) Nothing I did or didn't do caused this to happen; it just happened. Cosmic ray.

How you back up and how often depends on what you do. If you're working on your computer for several hours every day, you'll probably want to make daily backups. If you work only a couple of hours a week, make backups whenever you think you've done enough work that you don't want to lose.

Purists say make two backup copies, in addition to what's on your hard disk. Why? Consider this scenario. The file on your hard disk isn't working right, so you get out your backup copy and put it in your disk drive. What's wrong, though, is really with your disk drive, and it eats your backup copy. At this point you realize what's happening, but it's too late: your data's lost. If you have another backup copy, you still have your data. You can get your hard disk repaired and you'll still have your work.

> **Tip:** You hard disk is no "safer" than your floppy disks. It can crash, too. And if it does, you'll lose a lot more work than if a floppy disk goes bad.

> **Tip:** Keep your backup disks clearly labeled so that you can figure out what's on them weeks after you've made them.

What Are Backups?

Backups are *not* copies of the same file on the same disk. Backups are copies that are on a different disk or on another medium, such as magnetic tape, and that you store somewhere away from your computer. Then, if your office catches on fire or your computer "walks," your backups are somewhere else.

There are several different ways to make backups.

> **Tip:** Your programs may make automatic timed "backup" files that end in .BAK or .BK!. These aren't really backups; they're just extra copies of what you're working on. If they're on your hard disk and something goes wrong with it, they'll be wiped out, too. They're great if there's a power failure and you can get the last ten minutes or so of your work back, but they're not so hot in case of hard disk disaster.

- Choose Disk Copy from the Disk Utilities group in the Shell, or use the DISKCOPY command to make backup copies of entire floppy disks, like program disks that you buy or collections of clip art on disks.

- Choose Copy from the File menu in the Shell, or, at the command line use the COPY or XCOPY commands to copy just the files and directories that you want copies of.

- Choose Backup Fixed Disk from the Disk Utilities group in the Shell, or use the BACKUP command at the command line to back up a whole hard disk (take a "snapshot" of what's on it) and the RESTORE command (or Restore Fixed Disk) to restore those backed-up files, if it's ever necessary.

We'll look at all of these.

To make a backup copy of a program disk you've bought or an entire disk of files, use the Disk Copy command in the Shell's Disk Utilities group or the DISKCOPY command.

When you double-click on Disk Copy (or highlight it with the arrow keys and press Enter, if you don't have a mouse), you'll see a dialog box all set up for you, assuming that you want to copy the disk in drive A onto a disk in drive B. If that's what you want, fine.

```
┌──────────── Disk Utilities ────────────┐
│ ▦  Main                                 │
│ ▭  Disk Copy                            │
│ ▭  Backup Fixed Disk                    │
│ ▭  Restore Fixed Disk                   │
│ ▭  Quick Format                         │
│ ▭  Format                               │
└─────────────────────────────────────────┘
```

But what if you have only one disk drive? It's still OK. DOS will figure out that you have only one and will do the disk copy, prompting you to insert the original disk (called the **source disk**) and the one you're making the copy on (called the **destination disk**).

Your destination disk (the one that's going to be the new copy) doesn't have to be formatted. You can use a new disk right out of the box. DOS will format it as it goes along.

When the disk copy is done (you'll be taken out to DOS for this part, just as though you were using the DOS DISKCOPY command), you'll be asked if you want to make more copies. After you're done copying disks, press any key to return to the Shell.

You can't copy copy-protected disks or the files on them. To copy them, get a program like COPY II PC from Central Point Software.

The second way to copy all the files on one disk onto another disk is to use the COPY command. It has two advantages: it lets you copy what's on a disk in drive A onto a disk in drive B even if they're different sizes, and it also reorganizes the copied files so that DOS can find them faster (they may have been scattered all over the original disk because of the way DOS stores files).

Backing Up a Program Disk

Using Disk Copy

▶ **Tip:** *Put a label on your destination disk before you start! It's easy to get the source and the destination disks mixed up when you're asked to swap disks in and out of the drive.*

▶ **Tip:** *You can't do a disk copy of a 5.25-inch disk onto a 3.5-inch disk, and vice versa. Instead of using Disk Copy, use the Copy command and copy *.* (everything) from this disk in one drive to the disk in another drive, or use the XCOPY /S command if there are subdirectories on the disk (see the DOS Commands section for details about this one).*

Using the Copy Command

▶ **Tip:** *See the Directories chapter for more about copying files.*

To copy all the files on one disk to another (assuming there aren't any subdirectories), if the original's in drive A and the copy's to be in drive B, click on the drive A icon, choose Select All from the File menu (or press Ctrl-/) and then press F8 and enter *b:* in the To: box.

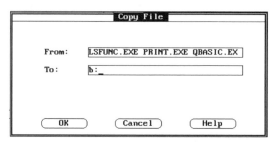

Remember, if you only have one disk drive, don't worry: DOS will figure it out and prompt you to insert the disk that's going to be the copy.

Backing Up a Hard Disk

▶ **Tip:** *If you're just copying a few files, use Copy. If you're copying entire directories and subdirectories, use XCOPY. It's discussed in the DOS Commands section.*

▶ **Tip:** *At the command line, use the BACKUP command.*

▶ **Tip:** *You can use unformatted disks with the BACKUP command; DOS will format them as it does the backup.*

The Backup Fixed Disk command (in the Disk Utilities group) is the one to use if you're backing up a whole hard disk and want a copy of everything that's on it.

If you're backing up a hard disk onto floppy disks, you'll need a good supply of them. Make sure you have enough before you start so that you don't have to run out and get more in the middle of a backup with your computer running. "Enough" is a *lot*: if you have a 20 Mb hard disk, you'll need about 57 360K (double-sided) floppy disks! Here's a rough estimate for the other sizes of floppies. For a 20 Mb hard disk, you'll need:

17 5 ¼-inch high-capacity (1.2 Mb) floppies *or* 28 3 ½-inch double-sided (720K) floppies *or* 14 3 ½-inch high-capacity (1.44 Mb) floppies.

To figure out how many floppies you need for your hard disk, assuming it's pretty full and that you're going to back up the whole thing, divide the capacity of your hard disk by the capacity of your floppies. So, with a 20 Mb hard disk and 360K floppies, that would be (roughly) 20,000,000 divided by 360,000. Round up if there's a fraction and then add another disk or two for hidden files.

Remember, this is a rough estimate, because K is really 1024, not 1000.

For a more accurate estimate, you can get a directory listing to find out the total number of bytes' worth of files that are going to be backed up; then divide that by the capacity of one of your floppy disks. Or use CHKDSK to see how much stuff is on your hard disk (subtract "bytes available" from "total disk space").

How many bytes are there per disk, if you want to be really accurate? Here it is:

Disk Size	Bytes
360K	368,640
1.2 Mb	1,228,800
720K	737,280
1.44 Mb	1,474,560

How can you check a disk's capacity? If it's a brand-new disk, it may be labeled. If you've used it before, though, the original label may have been covered over. Put the disk in drive A and press Ctrl-A (or click on the drive A icon). Then choose Show Information from the Options menu. Next to "Size" will be how many bytes are on the disk. You can compare it to the table above to get your disk's capacity. The number may not match exactly because of the way computers count.

Get out enough disks, labels for them, and a felt-tip pen. You'll be working with a lot of disks, and it's easy to lose track of them. You'll want to label each one as it's done. The BACKUP command numbers disks as 01, 02, 03, and so on, as they're made, and you have to restore them in the same order.

Here's how to back up a hard disk to floppies in drive A. Choose Backup Fixed Disk from the Disk Utilities group (if you're using the command line, the commands will be the same as those we're going to discuss here; just remember to type *backup* first.) You'll see a dialog box already filled out with the mysterious line c:*.* a: /s. That means "Back up everything on drive C from the root directory on down to the very last subdirectory, and use drive A for all the backup floppy disks." If that's what you want to do,

▶ **Tip:** *When to use what command to back up? Disk Copy for entire disks; Copy or XCOPY for files that will fit on one floppy disk; Backup Fixed Disk for an entire hard disk.*

▶ **Tip:** *You can also get a directory listing with DIR to check a disk's capacity, or use the CHKDSK command.*

Making the Backup

▶ **Tip:** *Delete all the files you don't want before you make a backup. You'll save yourself some time.*

▶ **Tip:** *Fixed disk? Hard disk? Same thing.*

fine. If you want to do something different, type over what's there and type in a different set of parameters and options. Here are a few examples:

▶ **Tip:** *See BACKUP in the DOS commands section for more information about these options.*

To back up just one directory (here, \OCT\REPORTS):

c:\oct\reports a:

To back up selected files in that directory (here, all files named SALES with any extension):

c:\oct\reports\sales.* a:

▶ **Tip:** *You can't delete files on a backed-up disk. You have to reformat it to reuse it. You can do a quick format on it, though.*

Normally the BACKUP command deletes any files it finds on the destination disk. If the disk in drive A already has files on it that you want to keep, enter it like this to back up all the files in REPORTS:

c:\oct\reports a: /a

Of course, you'd use the name of the directory you're backing up, not the one in the examples here.

To back up only the files that have been added or changed since the last time you backed up the directory, use the /a and /m options, like this:

c:\oct\reports a: /a /m

Restoring Backed-Up Files

Let's hope you won't ever have to restore your backed-up files and that you keep them only for insurance. If you do have to restore them someday, here's how to do it in the Shell. (The options you can enter are the same at the command line; just type *restore* first.)

Choose Restore Fixed Disk from the DOS Utilities group. DOS isn't giving you much help here; it just tells you to enter the source and destination drives and the parameters. If you're backing up disks from drive A to drive C, enter *restore a: c:*.* /s.* This says "Restore every file on the backup disk to its original place on drive C and even if the directory is no longer there, create it." This is probably how you'll use the command most often, if your hard disk has crashed and been repaired.

You can also restore files into selected directories. For example, to restore the files on the disk in drive A to the C:\OCT\REPORTS directory, enter the command as

a: c:\oct\reports*.*

One thing that can drive you nuts when you restore files is that you can sometimes get a message saying that DOS couldn't find any files to restore. You *know* those files are on that floppy disk, so something must be wrong with your computer, your files, DOS, or you. Not necessarily. It's just that DOS expects that you're going to restore backed-up files back into the same directory that you backed them up from. If that's not the case, it complains that it can't find any files to restore. To get around this, always give a directory name as the destination (where you want the files restored to) and add a *.* to indicate that you want all of the files restored. So if you had a disk full of backed-up files from C:\REPORTS\OCT in drive A, you'd restore them like we did in the example: *restore a: c:\reports\oct*.* *

If the current directory on drive C is the same one that you backed up from, you won't have this problem anyway.

Another neat option to use with RESTORE is the /p option, which tells DOS to prompt you before restoring each file. Consider this: you made your backup, but then you continued to do work on your hard disk, so some of the files that are stored on it are in fact more up-to-date than the ones on your backup disk. If you use the /p option and DOS comes across any of these files, it will prompt you about whether you really want to overwrite the more recent file with the older, backed-up version.

▶ **Tip:** *You can't copy files from a disk that you've used BACKUP on. You have to RESTORE them instead. If you've just made copies (with COPY, XCOPY, or DISKCOPY), you can copy them, though.*

▶ **Tip:** *You can restore files to a different hard disk than the one you backed up from.*

Getting Prompted

▶ **Tip:** *You can't restore copy-protected programs (like dBASE III). You have to reinstall them on your hard disk.*

Here's How To ...		
	Copy an entire floppy disk	Choose Disk Copy from the Disk Utilities group, or use the DOS DISKCOPY command
	Copy selected files or a single directory	Choose Copy from the File menu, or use the DOS COPY command
	Copy files in a directory and any of its subdirectories	Use the DOS XCOPY command
	Back up a hard disk	Choose Backup Fixed Disk from the Disk Utilities group, or use the DOS BACKUP command
	Restore backed-up files	Choose Restore Fixed Disk from the Disk Utilities group, or use the DOS RESTORE command

CHAPTER 9

Printing

Paper remembers so that you can forget.

Motto of the Nelson Printing Company, Spokane, Washington
Adolph Nelson, proprietor, circa 1933

You'll probably print most of the time by using one of your programs like Microsoft Word or Borland's Quattro Pro (I'm trying to be democratic by mentioning all sorts of programs), but there are ways to print directly from DOS.

Screen Dumps

You can get a copy of what's on your screen (called a **screen dump**) by pressing the Print Screen key. If you don't see a Print Screen key on your keyboard, look for one marked PrtSc. Press Shift and PrtSc at the same time to get a screen dump. Just make sure your printer's on and its "on line" light is lit before you do this, or your computer may hang up, and you'll have to restart it.

Printing a File

You can use the Shell's Print command or the DOS PRINT command to print text-only files (unformatted files).

In the Shell, choose Command Prompt from the Main group and give the PRINT command. Then return to the Shell and select the file or files you want to print. You can then choose Print from the File menu. The files will be added to the list of files that are being printed, called the **print queue.**

▶ **Tip:** *If you're going to print from the Shell, you have to first give the PRINT command at the command line, or Run it from the File menu.*

▶ **Tip:** *You can put the PRINT command in your AUTOEXEC.BAT file so that you can always immediately print from the Shell. See Chapter 10 for how.*

If you use the DOS PRINT command, you have more control over how a file is to be printed. You can specify which printer to use and see what's in the print queue, for example.

For example, to print a file named DEC.TXT by using the command line, enter the command as *print dec.txt.* You'll be asked for the name of the device you want to use; just press Enter to use your printer, if you've only got one.

Checking the Queue

To see what's in the print queue, just use the PRINT command by itself at the DOS command line, like this: *print.* DOS will show you a list of all the files that are scheduled for printing.

Choosing a Printer on Another Port

PRN means "the printer on the first parallel printer port," which is where most folks hook up their printer. If you have a printer connected to a serial port, like COM1, or if you have more than one printer, you'll need to tell DOS which port to use. There are two kinds of ports: **parallel ports** (called LPT1, LPT2, and so forth) and **serial ports** (called COM1, COM2, etc.). Dot-matrix printers commonly use parallel ports, and laser printers often use serial ports, but not always. Here's how to tell which port your printer is on (of course you could always look at the back of your computer, but mine is a bunch of spaghetti back there, and yours probably is, too).

▶ **Tip:** *You can print a bunch of files that have similar names by using wildcards.*

Turn your printer on. Then, at the DOS prompt, enter

copy con lpt1 (press Enter)

testing (press Enter)

Then press F6 and Enter. If it prints, you printer's on LPT1. If not, try LPT2, LPT3, COM1, COM2, and COM3 in the first line until the pesky thing prints. (With some laser or inkjet printers you may need to push the form feed button to get them to print.)

▶ **Tip:** *To cancel all printing, use the command PRINT /t.*

Now you know which port your printer's on. If it's not on LPT1, give the PRINT command like this, specifying which port your printer's on with the /d option:

print test.txt /d:com1 (use the name of your file instead of TEST.TXT).

If you want to print as you type at the keyboard, enter the command as *copy con prn* (CON is your console, or keyboard) and press Enter. Then type whatever you want the printer to print. When you've finished typing, press F6 and Enter. The printer will then start printing what you typed. (Try pressing the form feed button if it doesn't.)

Printing as You Type

		Here's How to ...
Get a printout of the screen	Press Shift-Print Screen	
Print a file or files	Use the DOS PRINT command at the command line; then you can use the File menu's Print command	
Cancel all printing	Use the PRINT /t command at the command line	
See what's in the print queue	Use the PRINT command at the command line	
Print as you type	Use the COPY command at the command line as *copy con prn*	

AUTOEXEC.BAT and CONFIG.SYS

> Knowledge is of two kinds: we know a subject ourselves,
> or we know where we can find information about it.
>
> Boswell's *Life of Dr. Johnson*, 1791

DOS uses two special files called AUTOEXEC.BAT and CONFIG.SYS each time you start your computer. They tell it which commands to execute as it starts up and prepare it to use the "devices," like a mouse or an extra disk drive, that you might have. Most of the time you don't have to know much about these special files. But there may be times when you *will* need to know something about them—if you buy new programs that want to change your AUTOEXEC.BAT file or if you get new hardware. You can look them up here then. Don't worry about them unless you have to, because some of this can get kind of technical.

AUTOEXEC.BAT

As part of its normal routine each time you start your computer, DOS checks a special file called AUTOEXEC.BAT and executes the commands that it finds in it. These commands usually include, at a minimum, the path of directories and subdirectories leading to where DOS and the programs you use most frequently are stored. You can put commands in your AUTOEXEC.BAT file that will do other things, such as make sure that everything you save is double-checked or set up a custom prompt for you instead of the standard C>.

▶ **Tip:** *The AUTOEXEC.BAT file executes whenever you start your computer, even if you restart it with Ctrl-Alt-Del.*

▶ **Tip:** *The .BAT means that this file is a special kind of file called a batch file. Batch files consist of commands that DOS executes, one right after another.*

▶ **Tip:** *Your AUTOEXEC.BAT file may be a lot more complex (or a lot simpler) than this one. If your system is running fine and you don't need to change it, don't change it!*

How can you tell whether you have an AUTOEXEC.BAT file? Easy. If your computer asks you for the date and time each time you start it, you *don't* have an AUTOEXEC.BAT; if it doesn't, you do. (If you're running DOS 5, you've got one, because Setup creates it.)

To see what's in your AUTOEXEC.BAT file by using the Shell, just highlight it (it'll be in your root directory) and press F9. (Or use the DOS TYPE command to see it by entering *type autoexec.bat* at the command line.) You'll probably see something like this, but yours won't be exactly like this one:

@ECHO OFF

PROMPT PG

PATH C:\;C:\DOS;C:\WP51

C:\DOS\DOSSHELL

These cryptic lines tell DOS not to display the AUTOEXEC.BAT file as it executes (the @ECHO OFF turns off the display); to set your prompt to show the path to the current directory (the PROMPT PG line); to let you run DOS commands and start WordPerfect 5.1 from any directory, even if you're not in the DOS or WP51 directories; and to start the Shell running each time you start your computer.

Changing Your AUTOEXEC.BAT File

You can add commands to your AUTOEXEC.BAT file by editing it with the Editor that comes with DOS 5 or editing it with your favorite word processing program. (If you use a word processing program, be sure to save the revised AUTOEXEC.BAT as a text-only file. See the Files chapter if you're not sure what this is.)

Using the Editor

To use the DOS Editor for changing your AUTOEXEC.BAT file, highlight it and then choose Editor from the Main group. You'll be prompted for the name of the file to edit. Enter *autoexec.bat* and press Enter.

```
┌─────────────────── Main ───────────────────┐
│ ☐  Command Prompt                        ↑  │
│ ☐  Editor                                   │
│ ☐  MS-DOS QBasic                            │
│ ▦  Disk Utilities                           │
│ ▦  Johnson Project                          │
```

In the Editor, you can use the arrow keys or mouse to move around, use the Backspace and Del keys to delete what's there, or use the Edit menu to cut, copy, or paste lines. Just remember that in the AUTOEXEC.BAT file, each command must begin on a new, separate line. To add a new line, just type it and press Enter. When you're done, you can just choose Save from the File menu to save the file as AUTOEXEC.BAT (the Editor always saves files as text-only files, so you don't have to worry about using a special procedure), or use the Save As command to save it under a different name. You'll see a tip for why you might like to do this later in the chapter.

Now let's look at some of the ways you might want to change your AUTOEXEC.BAT file.

▶ **Tip:** *Keep the line with the DOSSHELL command in it as the last line in your AUTOEXEC.BAT file so that all the other things you want to do, like loading your mouse, will be done first, before the Shell comes up.*

▶ **Tip:** *You might want to print out a copy of the way your AUTOEXEC.BAT file was before you change it so that you can see what you did if things go wrong and your computer doesn't start the way you intended.*

Creating a Custom Prompt

DOS's Setup program alters your plain-vanilla DOS prompt (C>) to show the current path to whatever directory you're in by adding the line

PROMPT pg

to your AUTOEXEC.BAT file. So if you're in a subdirectory called SPREADS under an EXCEL directory on drive C, your prompt looks like this:

C:\EXCEL\SPREADS>

There are quite a few other things you can do to customize your DOS prompt, such as putting your name or the current date in it. Here's how you'd do your name:

PROMPT Your Name$g

The $g represents the > symbol. I'd get a prompt like *Kay Nelson>* (here DOS will tell the difference between upper- and lowercase). Just enter PROMPT to get the standard C> back.

See the PROMPT command in the DOS Commands section for some more examples; most of them require you to use some pretty cryptic symbols.

Setting Up a Delete Tracking File

DOS 5 lets you set up a special delete tracking file that keeps track of all the files you delete so that you can get them back with the UNDELETE or UNFORMAT commands. This is a very, very valuable thing to have! Information about your deleted files will be recorded automatically if you put this line in your AUTOEXEC.BAT file:

MIRROR C: /ta /tc

This tells DOS to set up that tracking file for drives A and C. If you use a drive B (or D), add /tb (or /td) to the line. See the MIRROR command in the DOS Commands section for more details, if you want them, but this line is all you need.

Canceling AUTOEXEC.BAT Commands

▶ **Tip:** *If you always want to start with a program, put the command used to start it as the last line in the AUTOEXEC.BAT file. Otherwise it will start before AUTOEXEC.BAT finishes running. If you always want to start in the Shell, put the DOSSHELL line last.*

Instead of deleting a command from your AUTOEXEC.BAT file, you can just stop it from being used by starting the line it's on with a REM command (for "remark"). For example, you may have a line in your AUTOEXEC.BAT file that starts some memory-resident program running. Many of these programs take up a lot of memory, and you may not be using them as much now that you have the DOS 5 Shell. If you think that a memory-resident program might be making your computer run slower or be causing other problems, you can temporarily stop it from running by starting its command line in the AUTOEXEC.BAT file with REM. To reactivate the command later, all you have to do is delete the REM, save the file, and restart your computer. Since you can see the lines you've disabled, you don't have to remember what you did if you want to enable them again later.

▶ **Tip:** *You can run your changed AUTOEXEC.BAT file by typing* autoexec.bat *at the DOS prompt.*

For example, if you're running Windows, you'll probably want to start the memory-resident program named SideKick directly from Windows *after* you start Windows running. Just begin the line that has SideKick in it with REM to keep your AUTOEXEC.BAT file from starting it first.

Batch Files

Your AUTOEXEC.BAT file is a special kind of file called a **batch file.** A batch file is just a text file that ends in .BAT and consists of DOS commands, one per line. Writing a batch file lets you give DOS a set of instructions: "first, do this; then do that."

You can create other batch files with the built-in Editor, because it's designed to handle text-only files, and when you save a file with it, the file will automatically be a text file. DOS wants text, just text, and no formatting commands like those that word processing programs automatically put in.

Unfortunately, we don't have room here to go into too much detail about batch files. However, if you're interested in creating one that protects your AUTOEXEC.BAT from being altered, read on.

Most programs that you buy now come with their own installation programs that will automatically go into your AUTOEXEC.BAT file and change it to suit the way they run (they may ask you beforehand if it's all right to do this). They may want to add themselves to your PATH command so that you can execute them from any directory, or do some other technical things. Usually they'll rename your existing AUTOEXEC.BAT file as AUTOEXEC.OLD or AUTOEXEC.BAK, so you can go back and look at what's in the two files to see what the differences are. Normally what these programs do to your AUTOEXEC.BAT file is perfectly okay and even necessary if they're going to run properly, so leave the changes they make alone unless you're having trouble, like getting error messages about programs not running properly.

However, if you find that installation programs are changing your AUTOEXEC.BAT file in ways that you don't want them to, there's a way you can prevent them from doing that. First, get your AUTOEXEC.BAT just as you want it; then save it as STARTUP.BAT (use the Editor to make sure that no invisible formatting commands get into it). Then create another AUTOEXEC.BAT file that consists of just these two lines:

@ECHO OFF

CALL STARTUP.BAT

And save it as AUTOEXEC.BAT!

From now on, you can let installation programs alter your AUTOEXEC.BAT file as much as they want to. When the installation program is done, you can take a look at

▶ **Tip:** *Most word processing programs will let you create text-only files, but it won't be in the "normal" way that you create documents with the program.*

Warning: Your AUTOEXEC.BAT Can Get Changed

▶ **Tip:** *You can set up a different AUTOEXEC.BAT file to stop programs from changing the one you have!*

your AUTOEXEC.BAT file (the differences will be obvious, since it started out as just two simple lines) and either edit your STARTUP.BAT file to include the changes, or delete them.

CONFIG.SYS

▶ **Tip:** *If you ever need to change a line in your CONFIG.SYS file, be sure to save it as a text file (use the Editor to make sure). Restart your computer for the change to take effect.*

DOS also executes another file called CONFIG.SYS when it starts up. This is your system configuration file . It tells DOS what kinds of devices—like external disk drives or a mouse—are connected to your computer, how many files can be used at a time, and so forth. Normally, you'll never need to change this file. However, some auto-installation programs will go in and change it for you to suit the way they run, so it's a good idea to know that CONFIG.SYS is there and a little bit about it so that you can respond intelligently to those "Change CONFIG.SYS?" prompts.

Buffers

One of the most common things installation programs do is change the number of files and buffers allowed. A **buffer** is a part of memory (random-access memory, not disk storage space) that DOS uses to hold the information that it reads from disk. It's faster to read from RAM than from a disk, so having buffers lets DOS hold in RAM the information that's most likely to be needed next and access it quickly.

How many buffers should you have? If you've got a full 640K of RAM, probably 20 or 30. If you have a hard disk that's bigger than 80 Mb, you can use 40 or 50 buffers with no problem. It's best just to let the auto-installation programs set the number of buffers for you unless you look at your CONFIG.SYS file and see that you've only got 8, or some small number like that (unless you're using a disk cache, which does the same thing that BUFFERS does).

Files

FILES is another setting you'll see in your CONFIG.SYS file, and it's also one that you may be prompted about when those auto-installation programs run. The FILES statement tells DOS the maximum number of files to keep track of at one time. Some programs needs to have a lot of files open at one time—dBASE III+ likes to have 20, for example. If you start getting error messages about having too many files open, increase the FILES= number in your CONFIG.SYS file.

You'll probably see a few other commands in your CONFIG.SYS file, too. DEVICE= is a command that tells DOS what kind of hardware you're using. Normally, when you get a new piece of equipment, like a mouse or a disk drive, its installation program will put a DEVICE= statement in your CONFIG.SYS file so that DOS will know it's there. You'll usually never need to change these things.

Devices

▶ **Tip:** *What comes after the = is called a device driver program. It usually ends in .SYS, too. Now you know.*

Your computer, without doubt, has 640K of **conventional memory.** But it may have more memory than that. It gets complicated. In a nutshell, here's what you need to know:

If your system has extended memory, DOS can use part of it. Normally, the Setup program will be able to tell whether you have extended memory and will set DOS 5 up to use it. You can check to see that your CONFIG.SYS file has the lines

DEVICE = HIMEM.SYS

DOS = HIGH

If CONFIG.SYS doesn't have these lines and the MEM command tells you that you have extended memory, add these lines to your CONFIG.SYS file and save it (use the Editor). This will make more memory available to your programs.

Extra Memory

▶ **Tip:** *Use the MEM command to see what kind of memory you have.*

There are several different kinds of memory. You can skip this memory lane part if you don't care, or come back to it later when you want to know the difference between extended memory and expanded memory. (I always mix them up.) And you may never have to know.

Back when IBM invented the computer (ha), They decided that 640K of random-access memory (RAM) was the most anybody would ever need. But in their own typical IBM fashion, they left a whole megabyte of space for this 640K of conventional memory. Programs that run with DOS normally use conventional memory, and a lot of programs can't use any other kind.

The computer designers reserved the space between 640K and 1 Mb, which is 384K, because as you may or may not recall, 1 Mb is 1024K, the way computer people count.

More about Memory

In this 384K of **reserved memory,** they figured everybody would put video adapter memory for the displays you see on your screen. Well, it didn't work out that way: everybody needed more RAM but not that much video memory. But the hardware was set up so that programs couldn't store information in that area, and so it just sat there, unused, until DOS 5 came along. We'll get back to this fascinating bit of history in a minute.

▶ **Tip:** *Well ... if you had a special memory-management program, you could use it.*

In the meantime, folks were scrabbling to figure out how to get around the carefully designed built-in limitations of the hardware and add more memory to DOS-type personal computers. (Hey, the Macintosh started out with a big 128K of RAM, but the Apple people didn't box themselves in like the IBM/Microsoft folks did!) So they came up with **memory manager programs** to get around it. To use this new-style memory, called **expanded memory** and **extended memory,** you have to also use one of these memory manager programs (one comes with your extra memory when you buy it). DOS 5 also comes with two more memory managers for extended memory, maybe more, depending on how you're counting. You've seen how that counting stuff goes.

Expanded Memory

There are two kinds of extra memory that you can add. Expanded memory can be added to most computers. Extended memory—the other kind—can be added only to 286 and higher computers.

The way expanded memory works is a little tricky: memory in an added memory board just gets swapped in and out by a memory manager, like the con artist and the shell game. You can think of it as being there, but not in any given place. A lot of folks think that expanded memory is that 384K space above conventional memory, but it's not. You can have more than 384K of expanded memory, and your memory manager just swaps it around for you. DOS doesn't have any special manager for expanded memory; you just use the one that came with the added board. Some programs can use expanded memory; others can't.

Extended Memory

Most 286 and higher computers come with more memory than one megabyte, and that's called **extended memory.** It's above the 640K of conventional memory and the mysterious 384K that's sometimes called the upper memory block, reserved memory, or even (incorrectly) high memory. DOS has special managers for your extended memory.

Now the difference between extended memory and expanded memory is in how DOS and your programs use it. Instead of fooling programs about what memory they're really using like expanded memory does, extended memory actually changes the way the processor accesses memory. Think of it as extending its arm out to grab more memory all over the place. (That's oversimplified, of course, but why did they have to make it so *hard?*) Most of DOS 5 can go in and run in extended memory, leaving more of the other, conventional kind of memory available to your programs. And that's good.

Setup will automatically set you up to use extended memory, as we said earlier, with the extended memory manager that comes with DOS 5, called HIMEM.SYS. And it will load most of DOS into the **high memory area (HMA),** which is the first 64K beyond the 1 Mb line.

Got a 386? Read On.

Now it gets more complex. If I were you at this point I would close this book and get out the manual to get the gory details. But just to give you an overview, read on.

If you have a 386 or 486 computer, you can use a memory manager called EMM386 that comes with DOS 5. Setup doesn't automatically do anything with this one; you have to put it into your CONFIG.SYS file yourself with a line like

DEVICE = C:\DOS\EMM386.EXE NOEMS

EMM386 allows some of the extended memory to be used as expanded memory, for programs that can use ex-

> ▶ **Tip:** *Extended memory is the kind that Windows loves to use. You have to have a 286 or higher computer to use it.*

panded but not extended memory. But the NOEMS in the example line says "don't use expanded memory." If your programs can use it, you'll want to use the RAM switch instead of NOEMS and specify how much expanded memory to use, like 640 RAM to use 640K of expanded memory.

You can also use EMM386 to manage that unused memory in the upper memory block, the one that was designed in and then left alone. Once you've set DOS up to use it, you can load programs into it by using the LOADHIGH command (there are some examples of it in the DOS Commands section). The trick is that you've got to be using HIMEM and EMM386, both, for DOS to use the upper memory block. So if you've done all the stuff above and you've got HIMEM and EMM386 in your CONFIG.SYS file, add UMB to the end of the DOS = HIGH line, like this:

DOS = HIGH, UMB

Now that you've done all that, you can load programs into your high memory area, because DOS has been prepared to use it. Just get out the manual.

Logical Drives

▶ **Tip:** *Look up FASTOPEN in the DOS commands section for another way to speed up your computer.*

▶ **Tip:** *Logical drives are sometimes called virtual drives, too.*

What else might you see in a CONFIG.SYS file? LASTDRIVE tells DOS how many disk drives you have. Normally drives A and B are your floppy disk drives and C and D are hard disk drives. DOS throws in another one, just for fun: drive E, even if you don't have five disk drives. These don't have to be real, physical disk drives that you can touch: they can be "logical" drives. A logical drive is— well, it's one that doesn't physically exist but it acts as if it does (this is logical?). A RAM disk is an example of a logical drive. Network drives are also logical drives. If you add more hard disk drives to your system, you may need to increase the letter of the LASTDRIVE.

You may see other commands in your CONFIG.SYS file. These are special DOS commands that can't be entered on the command line (except for BREAK) but that tell DOS special things about your system.

One last thing that you may see in your CONFIG.SYS file is an INSTALL= statement. This is used to load four special memory-resident commands: FASTOPEN, SHARE, KEYB, and NLSFUNC. Those last two are for when you're switching from one international setting to another. FASTOPEN tells DOS how many files to keep track of, so it can speed up your system's performance, and SHARE is used when you're on a network.

Other CONFIG.SYS Commands

See what's in your AUTOEXEC.BAT or CONFIG.SYS file	Highlight it and press F9, or TYPE AUTOEXEC.BAT (or CONFIG.SYS) at the command prompt	**Here's How To ...**
Use the Editor	Choose Editor from the Main group in the Shell, or enter *edit* at the command prompt	
Set up a delete tracking file for drives A and C	Add this line to your AUTOEXEC.BAT file: MIRROR C: /ta /tc	
Cancel a command in your AUTOEXEC.BAT file	Start the line it's on with REM	
Create a batch file	Use the Editor and put one DOS command per line. Give the file a .BAT extension when you name it.	

DOS Commands

11

"I had it right, but I got it wrong."

LATE TWENTIETH-CENTURY COUNTRY/WESTERN SONG, AUTHOR UNKNOWN

DOS is very picky about how it wants you to enter commands. If you misspell a command, you'll get a "Bad command or file name" message. This doesn't mean that the command was bad, just that you probably typed it wrong. And DOS isn't always logical. For example, you can abbreviate the DELETE command as DEL, but you can't shorten the ERASE command (which does the same thing as DEL) to ERA.

This section will show you how to enter all the DOS commands just the way DOS wants them. It will also show you a lot of examples of how to use the options—those cryptic letters that are preceded by a slash that tell DOS how you want the command carried out.

▶ **Tip:** *There are other commands, like those for batch files, but this is a "little" DOS 5 book.*

Recall from Chapter 3 that a command consists of three parts: the command itself, followed (sometimes) by what you want it to act on (the parameters), followed (sometimes) by an option or two.

DOS doesn't care whether you use uppercase or lowercase, and for the most part, it doesn't care a lot about spacing. Just remember always to leave a space between the command itself and what follows it. But DIR /W /P is just the same as DIR /W/P (which is, of course, the same as *dir /w /p*). Don't worry about the spacing between options or whether letters are capitalized. I've capitalized the DOS commands themselves to distinguish them from the Shell commands that you can pick from menus.

Tip: *You can get help at the command line by typing* help *and the name of the command you want help on and pressing Enter.*

Sometimes you'll need to use a colon (:) with an option. Just look carefully at the examples. If you leave the colon out, you can get one of those rebuking messages.

If you've used DOS before, this section will help remind you of what to do so that you don't have to remember the picky little details. You'll see which commands are new in DOS 5 and those that were new in DOS 4, too, since so many of you decided not to use it.

APPEND

Use APPEND to specify the directories that contain files a program needs. It lets you run programs without having to change to the directories that contain them.

How to Enter It

APPEND directories to be searched

Examples

APPEND C:\LETTERS lets you use all the files in the \LETTERS directory just as if they were really in your current directory.

APPEND A:\MEMOS;B:\DOCS lets you use the files in a directory called MEMOS on drive A and a directory called DOCS on drive B as though they were in the current directory. Notice that the paths are separated by semicolons.

APPEND shows you all the directories that are currently appended.

APPEND ; removes the list of appended directories so that DOS searches only the current directory for files.

Details

APPEND is one of those commands that are used most often with older programs that don't let you put your program files in one directory and other files that the program needs in another. WordStar Release 3 is one of these.

Tip: *It's too bad that a lot of the "hard" DOS commands come at the beginning of the alphabet! If you're reading these commands in sequence, don't be scared off. There are a lot of simpler commands coming as soon as we get out of the A's.*

If you regularly use programs that need the APPEND command to find files in other directories, you can put it in your AUTOEXEC.BAT file along with the directories so that you don't have to type it again (APPEND C:\LETTERS, for example). See Chapter 10.

How is APPEND different from PATH? The PATH command lets you specify directories to be searched for executable files (programs); APPEND lets you specify data files. You should use PATH in your AUTOEXEC.BAT file, for sure.

There are some exotic options you can use with APPEND, but we won't go into detail about them here because you use them mostly if you're working with programming tools.

Use ASSIGN to fool DOS into thinking that one disk drive is actually another.

ASSIGN

ASSIGN one drive = another drive

How to Enter It

ASSIGN A = C B = C to run a program on drive C (your hard disk) even though the program's manual tells you you have to put your program disk in drive A and your data disk in drive B.

Examples

ASSIGN /STATUS shows your current assignments.

ASSIGN removes all assignments.

This command is used mainly with older programs that assume you have only floppy disk drives. It's similar to the SUBST command that lets you substitute a drive letter for a path to a directory.

Details

Note that you don't use a colon after the drive letter with ASSIGN.

Don't use ASSIGN with commands that need to know which drive you're really using (like BACKUP and RESTORE). And it won't work with copy-protected programs that want a disk to be in a certain drive.

Use ATTRIB to make a file read-only (protect it from being changed) or, during a backup or copy procedure, to mark which files have been backed up or copied.

ATTRIB

Choose Change Attributes from the File menu.

This icon means that it's usually easier to use the Shell instead of this command. In this case, you'd choose Change Attributes from the File menu.

How to Enter It　**ATTRIB options file name**

Examples　**ATTRIB +r REPORT.DOC** protects the file REPORT.DOC from being changed or erased, although you can read it. (The options +r and -r turn a file's read-only attribute on and off.)

▶ **Tip:** *You can use wildcards with ATTRIB.*

ATTRIB -r A:\REPORTS\OCT /S removes the read-only protection from the files in the REPORTS\OCT directory on drive A as well as from the files in any subdirectories under it. (The /S option specifies that all the files in any subdirectories are to be affected by ATTRIB.)

ATTRIB +a *.* turns on the archive attribute for all the files in the current directory (you'd add the /S option if you wanted to turn it on for all the files in any subdirectories, too). This makes sure that they will all be included in the next backup, whether they've been modified or not. (The options +a and -a turn a file's archive attribute on and off.)

ATTRIB EXAMPLE.DOC reports whether the read-only and the archive attributes are on or off for the file.

Details　DOS 5 added the options +s and -s, which let you set a file as a system file, but you probably don't want to do this anyway.

DOS normally turns on the archive attribute when you create or change a file. When you do a backup or copy a bunch of files with XCOPY, you may sometimes want to turn on the archive attribute for a file that hasn't been changed, so that it will be backed up or copied, too. You can also turn off the archive attribute for a file that has been changed if you don't want to include it in the backup or copy procedure. See BACKUP and XCOPY also.

Use BACKUP to back up files from your hard disk to floppy disks.

BACKUP source directory destination directory *options*

BACKUP C:\SPREADS*.* A: backs up all the files in the SPREADS directory on your hard disk C to floppy disks in drive A. You'll be prompted to insert more floppy disks as needed.

BACKUP C:*.* A: /S backs up everything on drive C to floppies in drive A. (The /S option backs up all subdirectories, too.)

BACKUP C:\SPREADS /S /D:9-28-91 backs up all the files in the SPREADS directory and files in any of its subdirectories that have been created or changed since September 28, 1991. (The /D option lets you specify a date. There's also a /T option that lets you specify a time. Note that you have to use a colon before the date and the time, too.)

BACKUP C:*.* A: /S /M backs up all the files on drive C that have been changed since the last time you made a backup. (The /M option specifies that only files that have been changed are used in the backup.)

BACKUP C:\BOOK\CH8 A: /A backs up CH8 onto a floppy disk in drive A: that presumably has chapters 1–7 already on it. (The /A option adds backed-up files to a backup disk without erasing any files that are already on it.)

BACKUP C:\SPREADS*.* A: /F:360 backs up all the files in the SPREADS directory to a floppy disk in drive A and formats the disk as a 360K disk. (The /F: option lets you specify that a disk be formatted to a special capacity; here, drive A is presumably a high-density drive but you want to format the backup disks as 360K.)

There's another option, /L, that makes a backup log showing the name of each file and the number of each disk it was backed up to. If you don't specify a file name, C:\BACKUP.LOG is used.

BACKUP

How to Enter It

Examples

Choose Backup Fixed Disk from the Disk Utilities.

▶ **Tip:** *Specifying a time without a date will get you a bunch of all sorts of files that you probably don't want!*

▶ **Tip:** *This is a fast way to make an incremental backup.*

▶ **Tip:** *Use the /A option if you're backing up files to a disk that already has files on it.*

Details   DOS labels backup disks as 01, 02, etc. You'll need to restore them in the same order, so label them.

▶ **Tip:** *You may want to use XCOPY instead of BACKUP. See XCOPY.*

You don't need to use formatted disks; BACKUP will format them (but see the example above if you want to format a disk in a different capacity than your disk drive).

Use COPY if you're copying just a few files.

Use RESTORE, not COPY, to restore backed-up files.

BREAK   Use BREAK to specify that you can press Ctrl-Break or Ctrl-C to stop a program any time it's running, not just during keyboard and screen operations, which is the normal setting.

How to Enter It   **BREAK ON, BREAK OFF** turns BREAK on and off; **BREAK** shows whether Break is on or not.

Details   Normally DOS interrupts, or breaks, when you press Ctrl-C only if an operation that uses the keyboard, screen, or printer is under way. If you turn on BREAK, processes like saving a file will be interrupted when you press Ctrl-C.

Most programs have a special way for you to stop them gracefully, without destroying any data that may be being saved. It's best to leave BREAK alone in most cases. The only logical reason I've ever heard of for using it is if you're testing programs of unknown origin and want an instant way to bail out if something starts going wrong.

CHCP   Use CHCP to change the code page (character set) your computer uses, or to display the code number for the character set that's in effect.

How to Enter It   **CHCP code page number**

Example   **CHCP 863** sets the current character set to French-Canadian.

It's not as easy as you think! CHCP is only one of several commands you use if you want to use DOS's international language support features. You first have to use the NLSFUNC command to tell DOS where a file named COUNTRY.SYS is (this file has the information about the date and time formats and special symbols for different countries). You then have to use the MODE command to prepare the code pages you want to be able to use and then select which one is to be active. You then have to load a new keyboard translation table with the KEYB command. (You still there?) *Then* you can use CHCP to switch between code pages. Better get somebody else to do it, or get out one of those thousand-page books and settle down for the evening.

Code 437 is U.S., 850 is Multinational, 860 is Portuguese, 863 is French-Canadian, and 865 is Nordic.

Details

▶ **Tip:** *You don't need to do any of this unless you're trying to use a PC bought in the United States for work in a language other than English.*

Use CD to change to a different directory.

CD path

CD \LOTUS changes your current directory to LOTUS.

CD displays the name of the current directory.

CD .. moves you up one level in the directory structure.

**CD ** takes you directly to the root directory.

If you want to change to a directory that's a subdirectory of the directory you're in, you don't need to type the backslash. For example, if you're in a directory named WINTER that has a subdirectory named DEC, you can type CD DEC.

One of the commonest mistakes you can make is to create a directory (with MD, for Make Directory) and then forget to change to it with CD.

The CD command doesn't change the current drive. To change the current drive, type A: or B: or C: at the DOS prompt (remember the colon).

You can also use CHDIR instead of CD, but why bother?

CD (CHDIR)

How to Enter It

Examples

Just highlight a directory in the Shell to change to it.

Details

▶ **Tip:** *Remember the shortcuts .. and \ (see the examples). They can save you time.*

CHKDSK   Use CHKDSK to check your disk to see how much free space is left on it, see how much RAM is available, and fix errors on the disk.

How to Enter It   **CHKDSK drive:** *options*

Examples   **CHKDSK** checks the current disk and reports its volume name, date of creation, storage capacity, number of files, amount of free space, number of bad sectors, and so forth.

CHKDSK A: checks the disk in drive A.

CHKDSK /F checks the disk and also "fixes" errors that it finds on the disk, like fragmented files, lost clusters, and bad sectors (these terms all refer to the way DOS physically stores data on the disk).

CHKDSK /V displays the name of each file as it's being checked.

Details   Using CHKDSK with the /F option locates bits of files that have been separated from the files they belong to (these are called "lost clusters"). If CHKDSK finds any of these, it asks you whether you want them converted to files. If you say Yes, it will convert those unusable bits of files to numbered files that end in .CHK, and you can then delete them all (DEL *.CHK) to get rid of them and free up more space on the disk. You can also look at them and see what they contain and try to figure out which file they belong to, but it's usually a waste of time, since they're probably unusable anyway.

   If you get the message "Convert directory to file?" it basically means that everything in the directory is garbage. (Converting it to a file may help you learn what *was* there, though.)

   If you give the command as CHKDSK *.*, CHKDSK will check to see whether files are contiguous (stored next to each other) or not. If they aren't, your disk operations are slower than they could be. You can speed up disk operations by using COPY (or XCOPY) to copy the files on the disk onto a different disk. (When files are copied, they are put back next to each other again, in the right order.) Don't use DISKCOPY, though, or you'll just transfer the problem from one disk to another!

▶ **Tip:** *Get out one of those thousand-page tomes if you want to find out about all the various kinds of problems that can happen to a disk.*

If you're optimizing your hard disk this way, don't use COPY or XCOPY; use BACKUP and then FORMAT the disk and RESTORE the backed-up files.

Don't panic if CHKDSK reports bad sectors. These are unreliable parts of the disk that were ignored when it was formatted.

▶ **Tip:** *Using CHKDSK /F can speed up disk operations by getting rid of file fragments.*

Use CLS to clear the screen and reposition the cursor in the upper-left corner.

CLS

CLS

How to Enter It

CLS just clears the screen; it doesn't affect anything that you've saved.

Details

You can also use CLS in batch files, if you need to present information on a new, blank screen, for example.

Use COMMAND to start another copy of DOS running.

COMMAND

COMMAND PATH *options*

How to Enter It

Sometimes you may want to start another copy of DOS running. For example, if you're doing programming in Pascal or BASIC or some other language, you may want to execute a couple of DOS commands while you're in your program, and you can do that with the COMMAND command. If it's likely that you're going to do this, though, you're probably not reading this book. I'll just mention that when you give the command, you'll need to supply the path to where the command processor (the copy of DOS) is, and that the options will let you specify a new environment size and all sorts of other technical goodies.

Details

Use COMP to compare two files.

COMP

COMP file1 file2

How to Enter It

Examples **COMP LETTER.DOC REPORT.DOC** compares the files character by character and reports the locations where the files are not alike. The first location is called OFFSET 0, and all the locations are given in hexadecimal notation, so COMP's not a whole lot of help except to let you know that two files aren't exactly alike.

COMP LETTER.DOC REPORT.DOC /L displays the line number where the differences occur.

Details If one file is longer than the other, DOS will just report that they're different sizes instead of comparing them character by character.

▶ **Tip:** *If you just type COMP, you'll be prompted for which files to compare.*

If COMP finds more than ten discrepancies, it stops comparing files.

DOS 5 adds the /A, /C, /D, /L, and /N options that let you specify whether the differences are displayed as characters (/A), are not case sensitive (/C), are displayed in hexadecimal (/D), are displayed as line numbers (L), or compares the first *n* lines (N:*number*). DOS 5 also has an FC command that does much the same as COMP and is easier to read.

COPY Use COPY to copy files. You can also use it to join files together.

How to Enter It **COPY source file *options* destination *options***

Examples **COPY OCT.RPT OCT.BAK** makes a duplicate of the file OCT.RPT with a .BAK extension, so that you'll know it's a backup copy. The copy is made in the current directory.

Choose Copy from the File menu or press F8.

COPY C:\SPREADS\OCT.RPT A: copies the OCT.RPT file, which is not in the current directory, to a disk in drive A, naming the copy OCT.RPT, its original name.

COPY A:*.* C: /V copies all the files in the current directory of the disk in drive A to the current directory on your hard disk (drive C). It also verifies that each copy was made correctly, with the /V option.

COPY CH? C:\LOTUS\REPORTS copies all files in the current directory starting with CH and ending in one character, such as CH1, CH2, CH3, and so forth, to the LOTUS\REPORTS directory on drive C.

COPY CON: DOIT.BAT creates a batch file named DOIT consisting of whatever you type next after pressing Enter. The CON: means "console," or keyboard, so what you're doing is copying from the keyboard. Press F6 when you're through typing; this tells DOS that it's the end of the file.

COPY OCT.RPT+NOV.RPT DEC.RPT combines the two files into a file named DEC.RPT. You can combine any number of files, not just two.

There are two exotic options, /A and /B. The first treats the file as if it were a text-only file, and the second treats it as a program (binary) file. You won't normally have to use the /A and /B options, but you may want to use /V to have DOS verify that each copy was made accurately.

Use COPY if you're copying only a few files, or files that have similar names, so that you can use the wildcards ? (for one character) and * (for any number of characters).

Use XCOPY if you're copying a large number of files, or if you want to copy files by date, or if you're copying entire directories and subdirectories.

Use DISKCOPY to duplicate disks.

Use BACKUP to back up large numbers of files on your hard disk to floppy disks in one of your floppy drives. You have to use RESTORE to put them back on the hard disk, not COPY.

Use REN to rename files.

Before you erase your original files, make sure that the copies are really where you thought you copied them by changing to that directory and getting a listing of what's in it with the DIR command.

It's easy to move or copy a file from one directory to another in the Shell, but to ,move a file at the command line, you have to COPY first and then DEL the original.

▶ **Tip:** *This is the way to create simple batch files quickly.*

Details

▶ **Tip:** *Other commands that let you use wildcards: ATTRIB, BACKUP, CHKDSK, COMP, DEL, DIR, ERASE, FIND, PRINT, RECOVER, REN, REPLACE, RESTORE, and XCOPY.*

▶ **Tip:** *If DOS won't let you copy to a floppy disk and you get a "write-protect error" message, remove the write-protect tab from the disk (it's over the notch on the side). For a 3.5-inch disk, slide the plastic tab over the hole (close it).*

Use CTTY to change your standard input device, which is usually the keyboard. You could connect another terminal to your computer, for example.

CTTY

How to Enter It CTTY device

Examples **CTTY COM3:** tells DOS to use a device connected to your COM3 port for input.

CTTY CON: returns control to your keyboard.

Details This is another command you probably won't use very often. One case where you might use it is to allow a machine connected via modem (on one of your COM ports) to provide input to your computer.

▶ **Tip:** *The CTTY CON: command has to be issued from the remote terminal, which is currently in control.*

Note how you have to use the colon in both of the examples.

DATE Use DATE to display the system date, or set it.

How to Enter It **DATE** tells you the system date; **DATE MM-DD-YY** lets you set the date (type the current date, not "mm-dd-yy").

Details You can enter DATE and then respond to the prompt by typing in a new date. If the date is OK, just press Enter.

When you type the date, you don't have to use leading zeroes to take up two spaces. For example, 2-6-91 is just as OK as 02-06-91. (If you type 00 as the year, DOS will assume it is the year 2000.) You can enter the year as 91 or 1991.

You can also use slashes or periods in the date: 2-6-91, 2/6/91, and 2.6.91 are all OK.

DOS keeps track of leap years and such, so you shouldn't have to set the date unless your system's clock batteries get low.

DEL Use DEL (or ERASE) to erase files.

How to Enter It DEL filename

DEL REPORT.DOC erases the file named REPORT.DOC in the current directory.

DEL C:\REPORTS\REPORT1.DOC erases the file REPORT1.DOC in another directory.

DEL A:\REPORT.DOC erases the file named REPORT.DOC on a disk in drive A:.

DEL *.DOC erases everything ending in .DOC.

DEL *.* erases everything in the current directory (you'll be prompted about whether you really want to do this).

DEL *.* /P erases the directory file by file, prompting you whether you want each file erased (new in DOS 4).

Deleted files aren't really removed from a disk; they're just marked as deleted, and DOS will eventually write over them. You can often get them back by using the UNDELETE command, if you think of it right away.

Examples

▶ **Tip:** *You can abbreviate DELETE as DEL but you can't shorten ERASE to ERA. DOS doesn't understand "DELETE," either. Use either DEL or ERASE. Very logical.*

▶ **Tip:** *Deleting everything in a directory doesn't delete the directory itself.*

Details

Use DELOLDOS to delete the previous version of DOS (it's in a directory called OLD_DOS.X) and save yourself some disk space.

DELOLDOS

DELOLDOS

How to Enter It

Use DIR to see what's in a directory and get information about what it contains.

DIR

DIR directory *options*

How to Enter It

DIR shows you the files that are in the current directory

Examples

DIR A: /P shows the files that are in the current directory of the disk in drive A: and pauses after each screen is filled. To see the next screen of files, press a key on the keyboard.

Just highlight a directory name to see what's in it.

▶ **Tip:** *You can use wildcards with DIR.*

DIR /W shows you a five-across list of the current directory's files. It leaves out most of the details and just shows file names.

DIR *.DOC lists all files ending in .DOC

▶ **Tip:** *To see if a file's in a directory without getting a whole directory listing, just type the file's name after DIR, like DIR OCT.RPT. If it's there, it will be listed. If it's not, you'll get a "File not found" or "Bad command or file name" message.*

DIR /O:N alphabetizes the directory listing (/O:-N will alphabetize it in reverse order). In addition /O:E and /O-E will alphabetize it (or alphabetize it in reverse) by extension, /O:D and /O-D will sort it by date, and O/:S and O/:-S will sort it by size. (These options are new in DOS 5.)

DIR REPORT3.DOC tells you whether the file REPORT3.DOC is in the current directory.

DIR A: /A displays only files that haven't been backed up. (The /A option in DOS 5 lets you display files that have certain attributes; here, A represents the archive attribute. See ATTRIB for what the other attributes are.)

▶ **Tip:** *Use DIR /P if you're looking at a directory with a lot of files in it. Otherwise, they'll just zip by.*

DIR /S (new) lists the contents of all subdirectories.

DIR /B (new) lists one file name per line, with no other information.

DIR /L (new) lists names in lowercase.

Details   When you get a directory listing, you'll see the date and time the file was last modified or created and its size in bytes. You'll also get a report on how many files were located and the amount of free space (in bytes) on the disk.

If you use the /W option, you'll just see file names and the names of any subdirectories, plus the number of files and the amount of free space.

The notations . and .. at the beginning of a directory list are always there, even in an empty directory.

▶ **Tip:** *To change to a different drive, type its letter followed by a colon, like A: to change to drive A.*

Use the TREE command if you want to see the directory structure itself.

To change to a different directory, use the CD command.

DISKCOMP   Use DISKCOMP to compare two floppy disks.

How to Enter It   **DISKCOMP drive1 drive2** *options*

DISKCOMP A: B: compares the floppy disk in drive A with the one ion drive B.

DISKCOMP A: A: (or just DISKCOMP) compares two floppy disks, both in drive A. You'll be prompted to insert the second disk. Use this format if you have only one floppy drive of a given type.

Examples

▶ **Tip:** *It doesn't matter what order you put the disks in.*

Use DISKCOMP after you've done a DISKCOPY, to make sure that the copy was exact. If you user DISKCOMP after just copying files, the disks probably won't compare exactly, even though the copies are fine, because DOS will have put the files into different tracks on each disk.

There are two options, /1 and /8. /1 compares just one side of a double-sided disk, and 8 compares only 8 sectors per track on the disk. You'll probably never need to use these options.

DISKCOPY will only compare disks that have the same capacity.

Details

Use DISKCOPY to copy entire disks.

DISKCOPY source target

DISKCOPY A: B: copies the disk that's in drive A onto a disk in drive B.

DISKCOPY A: A: (or just DISKCOPY) copies a disk onto another disk if you have only one floppy drive, or if you have one 5.25-inch drive and one 3.5-inch drive (you'll be prompted to insert the source and target disks as needed).

DISKCOPY A: B: /V verifies that the copy was correctly made (new in DOS 5).

The *source disk* is the one you're copying. The *target disk* (also called the *destination* disk) is the new copy.

You can't DISKCOPY a hard disk. Change to a floppy drive (either A: or B:) before using DISKCOPY.

DISKCOPY is the same (well, almost the same) as COPY *.*, which means "copy everything." For example, if you

DISKCOPY

How to Enter It

Examples

Choose Disk Copy from the Disk Utilities.

Details

▶ **Tip:** *Label your source and target disks before you start so that you can tell them apart. It's easy to get mixed up halfway through copying!*

▶ **Tip:** *You can use an unformatted disk as the target disk.*

have a disk in drive A and you want to copy all the files that are on it (and there are no subdirectories) to a disk in drive B, you'd enter COPY *.* B:. OK, so when do you use DISKCOPY and when do you use COPY? Well, with DISKCOPY, the source and target disks have to be the same size. You can't DISKCOPY a 5.25-inch disk onto a 3.5-inch disk. So here's where you'd use COPY (or XCOPY) instead. Or if you just want to copy a few files, not everything on the disk, you'd use COPY (or XCOPY *.* /S if there are subdirectories on the disk).

DOSKEY

DOSKEY, new in DOS 5, starts a program that lets you recall DOS commands and create macros.

How to Enter It DOSKEY

Details Usually, when you give commands to DOS at the command line, you give them one at a time. DOS 5 has a new program called Doskey that lets you give several commands at once. It also tells DOS to remember what you did so that you can do it again without having to enter the commands from scratch. If you're a diehard command line fan, you'll love this feature.

Doskey isn't normally present when you start your computer. To put it in memory, type *doskey* at the command line. After it's loaded, you can type several commands at once, separating each with a Ctrl-T, which puts a paragraph mark (¶) on your screen.

Doskey keeps a list of all the commands you enter, and all you have to do is press F7 to see it. You can then choose which command you want to use again from this list by highlighting it and pressing Enter, or by pressing F9, typing the number of the command, and pressing Enter.

Doskey also lets you define macros. A macro is simply a set of instructions that you want to give to DOS. Defining macros is just slightly different from using Doskey the way you just did. Instead of separating commands with Ctrl-T, you use a dollar sign and T ($T).

Unfortunately, we don't have enough room to discuss everything Doskey can do here, as it's rather advanced.

Use DOSSHELL to start the Shell, if it doesn't start automatically when you turn on your computer.

DOSSHELL

DOSSHELL

How to Enter It

You can use the /T option to run the Shell in text mode, /G to run it in graphics mode, and /B to run it in black and white if you have a color monitor.

Details

Use EDIT to start the DOS 5 Editor, which allows you to edit text-only (ASCII) files.

EDIT

EDIT

How to Enter It

The Editor, new in DOS 5, is a full-screen text editor. It's included in addition to the notorious DOS editor called EDLIN, which let you edit only line by line. See the AUTOEXEC.BAT chapter for a peek at how to use the Editor.

Details

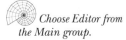 *Choose Editor from the Main group.*

See DEL; it's the same thing.

ERASE

Use EXIT to return to the original command processor you were working with if you used the COMMAND command.

EXIT

EXIT

How to Enter It

If you started another version of DOS running (with COMMAND), EXIT lets you get back to the "original" DOS.

Details

You'll sometimes type *exit* at the command line for other reasons. Some programs let you "exit to DOS" to carry out file management tasks like copying and formatting disks. To return to the program when you're through, type *exit.*

▶ **Tip:** *Also, if you exit temporarily from the Shell to the DOS prompt (with F3), you get back by typing* exit.

EXPAND   Use EXPAND to expand a compressed DOS 5 file.

How to Enter It   **EXPAND sourcefile targetfile**

Examples   **EXPAND A:DOSSHELL.EX_ C:\DOS\DOSSHELL.EXE**
uncompresses the DOSSHELL.EX_ file and stores it in
your DOS directory on your hard disk.

EXPAND A:*.EX_ C:\DOS uncompresses all the compressed files that have an .EX_ extension on the disk in
drive A to your DOS directory on drive C.

Details   DOS 5 comes as compressed files. (A compressed file has
a _ as the last character in its extension.) Normally, Setup
uncompresses all these files when you install DOS. However, if you ever need to expand just one or a few
of these compressed files, you can use the EXPAND
command.

FASTOPEN   Use FASTOPEN to let DOS keep track of where the files you
most recently used are, so that it can find them again quickly.

How to Enter It   **FASTOPEN drive:=number of files to keep track of**

Examples   **FASTOPEN C:=100** tells DOS to keep tracks of the last 100
files you opened on drive C. (It will handle up to 999 files).

▲**Warning:** *Don't run*
FASTOPEN from the Shell,
or your computer may
freeze up.

FASTOPEN C: tells DOS to keep track of 34 files, the default.

FASTOPEN C:=100 /X tells DOS 5 to use expanded
memory, saving conventional memory for your programs.

Details   This is a command that should go in your CONFIG.SYS
file if you have a complex structure of directories and
subdirectories. It speeds up disk access on a hard disk.
You'd enter it there like this:

INSTALL=C:\DOS
FASTOPEN.EXE C:=100

Use FC to compare two files and display what their differences are.

FC file1 file2 *options*

FC C:OCT.RPT A:OCT.RPT compares the two files and reports the lines that are different in them, followed by the first line that matches.

FC C:OCT.RPT A:OCT.RPT /N displays the line numbers.

FC is like COMP, but it's a lot easier to read FC's output.

It will zip by pretty fast on the screen, so press Ctrl-S to stop the display. Ctrl-C will stop it altogether.

FC assumes that you're comparing text files unless you give it one of the many rather exotic options (we won't go into them here) that tell it to compare binary (program) files, and so forth.

Use FDISK to create partitions on your hard disk (divide it into smaller "logical" disks).

FDISK

Typing FDISK starts a menu-driven program that lets you partition your hard disk, or divide it into two or more "logical" drives (drives that aren't physically separated but can be used as if they were. This is, believe it or not, logical to DOS). For example, I have an 80-Mb hard disk that's divided into two drives, C and D, mainly because my husband wants to use his own filing system and doesn't like mine. (Drive D is his.)

⚠Warning: *All data on your hard disk is destroyed when you use FDISK.*

Other people may want to run another operating system, such as UNIX, on their hard disk; partitioning the disk can let you have DOS on one drive and UNIX on another.

▶ **Tip:** *First, create your partitions with FDISK. Then format the newly created drives.*

If you've been using version 3.3, you'll be glad to know that starting with DOS 4, you can use a hard disk of any size without having to partition it.

FIND   Use FIND to locate a specific word or phrase in a group of files.

How to Enter It   FIND "word or phrase" *options* filenames

Examples   **FIND "Creative Solutions" LETTER1.DOC LETTER2.DOC** searches the files LETTER1.DOC and LETTER2.DOC in the current directory for the phrase *Creative Solutions* and displays the lines containing the phrase.

FIND "Brigette" /N C:\REPORTS\OCT.TXT NOV.TXT DEC.TXT searches three files in the C:\REPORTS directory and displays the lines as well as the line numbers the name occurs on (the /N option does that for you).

FIND "Brigette" /C C:\REPORTS\OCT.TXT counts the number of lines that have the word or phrase.

FIND "I said, ""Silence!"""" ACT1 ACT2 ACT3 searches the files for a phrase that uses quotation marks. Notice that you use two sets of quotation marks to do this.

▶ **Tip:** *Use the /N option to display the line number of the lines that have a match.*

FIND /V "408)" CLIENTS would search a phone list in a file named CLIENTS for all phone numbers that are *not* in the 408 area code (assuming the area codes are set up as (408) 555-1212). (The /V displays lines that *don't* contain the word or phrase you're looking for. You can use both /C and /V together to get the number of lines that don't have the matching pattern.)

Details   This is a handy command to use when you don't know the name of the file you're looking for, but you know that it's got a certain word in it—maybe the name of a company, or a personal name.

▶ **Tip:** *FIND won't let you use wildcards.*

It matters whether you use uppercase or lowercase letters with this command; FIND will find *Ralph* if you enter "Ralph" but not if you enter "ralph". (Use the /I option to make the search not case-sensitive.) However, it perversely doesn't care about spaces; if you enter "book" it will find *book, books, bookman, bookish,* and so forth.

FORMAT   Use FORMAT to prepare disks so that you can use them.

FORMAT drive: *options*

FORMAT A: formats a disk in drive A.

FORMAT A: /S puts hidden system files on the disk so that it can be used as a startup disk. (If you have a hard disk, you'll probably never use this one except to make an emergency startup disk.)

FORMAT A: /F:360 formats a disk in a high-capacity (1.2 Mb) 5.25-inch drive as a 360K disk (new in DOS 4). If you're planning to use the disk with a computer that has only a 360K drive, like an XT, do your formatting on the machine with the regular-capacity drive. The high-capacity drive will be able to read it just fine. Sometimes 360K disks formatted in high-capacity drives aren't readable when you get them in a regular-capacity drive.

FORMAT B: /F:720 to format a 3.5-inch disk in a high-capacity (1.44 Mb) drive as a 720K disk so that it can be used in a 720K disk drive (new in DOS 4). In DOS 3.3, to do the same thing, use FORMAT B: /N:9.

FORMAT A: /Q does a quick format on a disk in drive A that's been formatted before (you can't change the disk's formatted capacity with the /F option if you use this one). This is the same as a Quick Format in the Shell.

FORMAT A: /U does an "unconditional" format that won't let you use the UNFORMAT command on the disk (see UNFORMAT). These last two are new in DOS 5.

/1, /4, and /8 are options that let you format a disk as single sided (/1), format a 360K disk in a high-capacity (1.2 Mb) drive (/4), or format a 360K disk as 8 sectors per track (/8), used only with very old versions of DOS. You probably won't ever use any of these.

Formatting a disk destroys everything that's on it. With DOS 5, if you haven't used the /U (unconditional) option, you can sometimes get the data back, though (see UNFORMAT).

After you format a disk, you'll be prompted for a label. You don't have to use one; you can just press Enter instead. Using

How to Enter It

Examples

▶ **Tip:** *Format disks for the smallest-capacity drive they'll be used with.*

Choose Format or Quick Format from the Disk Utilities.

▶ **Tip:** *Don't FORMAT your hard disk unless you really want to wipe out everything on it.*

▶ **Tip:** *There's also a /B option that just makes a bootable disk but doesn't put DOS on it.*

Details

▶ **Tip:** *Don't use these characters in a disk label: + = / [ ] : ; , ? * \ < > |.*

▶ **Tip:** *The advantage of quick formatting is that it lets you clear off all the files, directories, and subdirectories on a disk without having to repeatedly DEL everything in a directory and them RD (remove) the directory.*

a label can help you identify and organize your disks, though. You can use spaces in volume (disk) labels and use 11 characters, so they don't have to be as cryptic as file names.

After the formatting is done, you'll also see a whole lot of numbers that tell you how much space is available on the disk. This space is reported in bytes, which can be confusing. See the Disks chapter for some tricks to help you tell what's what.

DOS will also report if there are any bad sectors on the disk. If there are, you can probably use the disk for storing files, but don't use it for copying disks with DISKCOPY or for making important backup disks of programs.

GRAFTABL

Use GRAFTABL only if you have a color graphics adapter (CGA) and are switching to different multinational character sets.

How to Enter It   **GRAFTABL** *options*

Examples   **GRAFTABL 860** loads display support for the Portuguese character set (code page number 860) (see CHCP for a list of the numbers).

GRAFTABL /STA displays which code page is in effect.

Details   This is another one you won't use very often. You'd use it only if you were switching to another language display (see CHCP for a review of what's required here).

GRAPHICS

Use GRAPHICS if you want to print graphics screens.

How to Enter It   **GRAPHICS** *printer* *options*

Examples   **GRAPHICS** lets you print graphics screens on black-and white printers.

GRAPHICS COLOR4 /B lets you print graphics screens on a color printer with an RGB ribbon, printing the background in color.

Normally you can print an image of what's on the screen (called a screen dump) by pressing Shift-PrtSc. However, graphics screens are a little different from normal text screens. If you're displaying graphic images, you won't be able to print them unless the GRAPHICS command has been issued.

To use GRAPHICS, you need to have a file named GRAPHICS.COM in the current directory. If it isn't there, give its path in the command (like C:\DOS\GRAPHICS).

If you print a lot of graphics screens regularly, put the GRAPHICS command in your AUTOEXEC.BAT file.

Oh, boy, there are a lot of options with this one. But you probably only have one printer, so you'll only use one of this impressive array: /B to print the background in color (on a color printer), or /LCD to print a liquid crystal display (like those used in some laptops), or /PRINTBOX:ID to select the size of the print box. For ID, enter either *std* (full size) or *lcd* (an exact-size screen from a liquid crystal display).

You can also use /R to print white on black (like what you see on the screen, but this eats up ribbon).

Your printer is one of these: COLOR1 (color printer with a black ribbon); or COLOR4 (color printer with a red, green, blue, and black ribbon); or COLOR8 (color printer with a cyan, magenta, yellow, and black ribbon); or HPDEFAULT, DESKJET, LASERJET, LASERJETII, PAINTJET, QUIETJET, QUIETJET PLUS, RUGGED-WRITER, RUGGEDWRITERWIDE, THINKJET, THERMAL, GRAPHICS, or GRAPHICSWIDEIBM printers (includes IBM Graphics Printer, Proprinter, or Quietwriter).

Details

▶ **Tip:** *You won't see graphics on your monitor unless you have a graphics display adapter in your system. If you do, your monitor will be called an EGA, VGA, PGA, or CGA (that G's for Graphics).*

Use HELP to get help about DOS 5 commands

HELP command or **command /?**

Entering either HELP XCOPY or XCOPY /? gets you help on the XCOPY command.

HELP

How to Enter It

Examples

JOIN Use JOIN to fool DOS into thinking that two disk drives are actually one.

How to Enter It **JOIN drive: directory**

Examples **JOIN A: C:\SALES** joins drive A to the (empty) SALES directory on drive C, so you can use the files on both drives A and C as though they were all on drive C.

▶ **Tip:** *You have to use an empty directory when you join a drive to it.*

JOIN A: /D removes the join so that drive A is treated as a separate drive again.

Details Why would you want to use JOIN? Well, it can save you some typing time if you're using a lot of files from the disk in drive A because you don't have to change to different drives and type long paths; you can just type the file names instead.

▶ **Tip:** *Don't use any of the commands that need to know where a disk really is—like BACKUP—with the JOIN command.*

The directory you're joining the drive to must be at the root level, as in the example.

KEYB Use KEYB to select a different keyboard layout.

How to Enter It **KEYB key code, code page, file name**
(Key code is a two-letter code for the country (like FR for FRANCE); code page is the code page number of the character set you're using (see CHCP); and file name is the path to the keyboard definition file (KEYBOARD.SYS), which has all of the keyboard translation tables.)

Example **KEYB FR,850\DOS\KEYBOARD.SYS** loads the French keyboard translation table based on code page 850 (multinational) and tells DOS that the KEYBOARD.SYS file is in the DOS directory.

Details This is another one that you won't use very often. It's the last step in setting up your computer to work with other languages and different keyboard arrangements (the

French use an AZERTY keyboard instead of the QWERTY keyboard). See CHCP for an overview of what's involved.

Once you have set all this up, you can switch between your chosen foreign-language keyboard and the standard U.S. keyboard by pressing Ctrl-Alt-F1. Ctrl-Alt-F2 returns you to the foreign-language keyboard.

Use LABEL to create or change the volume label on a disk

LABEL

LABEL drive:label

How to Enter It

LABEL A:june sales labels the disk in drive A as "june sales."

Examples

LABEL prompts you for the label you want to enter.

LABEL A: removes the disk label.

When your format a disk, you're asked if you want to use a volume label to help you keep track of what's on the disk. You can give the disk a name of up to 11 characters, including spaces (see FORMAT for the characters you can use). If you're not formatting a disk, you can use the LABEL command to change a disk's label or give it one, if it doesn't have one.

Details

Once a disk has a label, you'll see it whenever you get a directory listing. You can also see what a disk's label is by using the VOL command.

Use LOADHIGH to load a program into upper memory (a special kind of memory on a 386 or 486 computer).

LOADHIGH

LOADHIGH program

How to Enter It

Before you can use LOADHIGH (it can be abbreviated L), you need to do a couple of things. First, you have to have a 386 or 486 computer. Then you have to put the lines DEVICE = C:\DOS\EMM386.EXE and DOS = HIGH, UMB in your CONFIG.SYS file.

Details

Once you've done that, you can load programs into the 384K or so of memory that's usually reserved for your video display and other things—whatever's left over after everything's running. Those are the mysterious UMBs—upper memory blocks. DOS itself will load into extended memory.

MD (MKDIR)

Use the MD command to create a new subdirectory.

How to Enter It **MD path directoryname**

Examples **MD \SPREADS** creates a new subdirectory named SPREADS under your root directory.

MD A:\SPREADS creates a new subdirectory under the root directory on drive A.

Details If you want the new subdirectory under your current directory, you can omit the backslash. For example, if you were in a directory named LOTUS, you could create a SPREADS subdirectory by typing MD SPREADS.

Choose Create Directory from the File menu.

You can specify several different levels with the MD command. For example, MD C:\LOTUS\SPREADS\OCT\ SALES will create the SALES subdirectory (you can only create one subdirectory at a time.)

When you make a new directory, you don't automatically change to it. Use the CD command to change directories. It's a lot easier in the Shell.

To remove a directory, first use DEL to erase all the files in it. (You won't be able to delete the files represented by . and .., but that's OK.) Then use the RD command to remove the directory. You can't remove the current directory, so get out of it (typing CD .. will take you up one level) before you RD it.

MEM

Use MEM to see how much free memory you have.

How to Enter It **MEM *options***

MEM gives you a report of how much total memory you have (in bytes), how many bytes of it are available, and how much expanded and extended memory you have, and **MEM /C** will show you how your programs are using memory.

What's the difference between all these different kinds of memory? DOS basically recognizes 640K of conventional memory. However, if you have an 80286 computer (like an IBM AT), you have 1 Mb of memory. That extra 384K of memory is called expanded memory, and programs that were developed specifically to use it, like Lotus 1-2-3, can use it. (If you're wondering how this all adds up, it's because 1 Mb is 1024K.) Expanded memory is extra memory that you can purchase and use with an expanded memory manager; it will run even on 8086 and 8088 computers like an IBM XT. In any case, DOS keeps on thinking that you have only 640K of memory, because that's all it was designed to deal with.

Most 286 and higher computers come with more memory than one megabyte, and that's all called extended memory.

This command was added in DOS 4.

There are a couple of exotic options you can use with MEM. /PROGRAM displays which programs are in memory, and /DEBUG displays detailed information about the programs and memory usage.

Use MIRROR to record information that lets you use the UNFORMAT and UNDELETE commands.

MIRROR

MIRROR *options*

How to Enter It

MIRROR saves a record of what you do on the current drive.

Examples

MIRROR C: /TA /TC sets up delete records for both drives A and C.

MIRROR /U unloads the delete tracking program.

Details   When you use the MIRROR command, DOS 5 saves information about the files on your disk in a file called a delete tracking file, to make it easier to get the files back later with the UNDELETE or UNFORMAT commands.

If you want to always have the best chance of getting deleted files back, put the line MIRROR C: /TA /TC in your AUTOEXEC.BAT file so that you'll always have a delete tracking file. Add /TB if you use drive B, too.

▶ **Tip:** *This is a good thing to do even if you don't have partitions— actually, you have one big partition. Do it before you have trouble with your hard disk.*

If you're using a hard disk that's been subdivided into smaller sections called partitions, or logical drives, you can use the MIRROR command to get your partitions back, if they're ever lost. (You'll know they're lost if you try to use drive D or drive E and you get the message "Invalid drive specification.") To do this, make a copy of your partitioning information onto a floppy disk by entering the MIRROR command as *MIRROR /PARTN*. You'll be prompted to use a formatted disk, so have one handy.

See UNDELETE, too.

MODE   Use the MODE command to see the status of the things you've connected to your computer, to reconfigure a printer for a different port, to select another display monitor, to adjust the keyboard's key repeat rate, to prepare your monitor and keyboard to use different character sets, and to redirect printer output from one port to another.

Examples   **MODE CON** (an option new in DOS 4) shows you the status of your keyboard.

MODE LPT1:=COM1: redirects output from your first parallel printer ports (LPT1) to the first serial port (COM1).

Details   Most of the time, you won't have to use this command. It's an advanced command that has many different uses. Unless you're involved in things like changing your video display from 25 lines by 80 columns to 43 lines by 80 columns, you'll never have, or want, to use it. If you do get the urge to use MODE, curl up with one of those doorstop-sized books.

Use MORE to see files one screen at a time.

MORE

MORE < filename

How to Enter It

MORE < READ.ME displays the contents of the READ.ME file one screen at a time.

Example

When you finish reading each screen, press any key on the keyboard to see the next screen.

Details

The MORE command acts as a filter; that's why you have to use the < symbol with it. If you forget to put that symbol in, MORE will just echo back whatever you type at the keyboard or show you a blank screen if you press Enter. Very annoying. Press Ctrl-C to get out of this situation.

Press F9 to see what's in a highlighted file.

You can also view files one screen at a time with TYPE READ.ME | MORE. (That's another special symbol called a pipe.)

This is a useful way to read those "READ.ME" files that zip past you on the screen too fast to read. MORE them instead of TYPEing them.

▶ **Tip:** *MORE won't work on disks that are write-protected.*

If you try to read a program file (one that ends in .COM or .EXE) with either MORE or TYPE, all you'll see is garbage.

Use NLSFUNC to load support for different date, time, and currency formats for other countries and to enable you to switch among different character sets.

NLSFUNC

NLSFUNC path to COUNTRY.SYS file

How to Enter It

NLSFUNC C:\DOS\COUNTRY.SYS

Example

NLSFUNC (national language support) needs to know where a file named COUNTRY.SYS is. It contains all the different date and time format settings for various countries.

Details

Normally you won't need to use this one, but if you want an overview of how it works with other commands, see CHCP.

PATH

Use PATH to tell DOS which directories to search for program files, so that you don't have to change to the directory that contains a program before you can run it.

How to Enter It **PATH drive:\directories; drive:\directories**

Examples **PATH** displays the path to the directory where you are.

▶ **Tip:** *Don't use any spaces in the path. DOS stops reading when it gets to a space.*

PATH C:\;C:\DOS;C:\WP51 sets the search path as first, the root directory; then the DOS subdirectory; and then the WP51 subdirectory.

Details

▶ **Tip:** *The PATH command is normally used in your AUTOEXEC.BAT file.*

To add new programs to your path, use the DOS 5 Editor or your favorite word processing program in ASCII text mode (see the AUTOEXEC.BAT chapter for details). When you type the path, remember to use a semicolon to separate each path. Use a colon after your drive letter. Use a backslash between directories.

PRINT

Use PRINT to print a text file (ASCII file) while you're doing other work.

How to Enter It **PRINT** *options* **filename**

Examples **PRINT LETTER2** prints LETTER2 (you'll be asked which device to use; just press Enter to use your first printer port.

Type print *at the command line and then choose Print from the File menu.*

PRINT LETTER? prints all files beginning with LETTER and ending in any one character (like LETTER2, LETTER3, etc.)

PRINT LETTER3 /C cancels printing LETTER3 (the /C cancels printing the file you specify).

PRINT /T cancels all printing.

PRINT shows the status of the print queue.

The other options /B, /P, /Q /U, /S, and /M specify details like buffer size that you'll probably never use.

Details Most programs nowadays let you print while you're working on another document, so you may never have to use this command either. However, you can use PRINT to print on whatever printer is connected to your computer.

A neat use of the PRINT command is to let you print documents on a computer that doesn't have your word processing program on it. Suppose you've worked on a document in WordPerfect at home and you want to print it on a computer at work that doesn't have WordPerfect on it. You could take all your WordPerfect disks to work, install the program, and print your document, but using PRINT's a faster way. After you have your document formatted the way you want it, print it to disk. Printing to disk produces a formatted ASCII file that PRINT can recognize and use, and you can magically print the document from a computer that isn't running your word processing program.

Most word processing programs have a procedure that lets you do this, but you may have to dig it out of the manual, and it may be fairly complex. (Hint: in WordPerfect, with the document on screen, call up the Print menu, Select the printer the document's been formatted for, Edit it, select Port and Other, name the document with the name you'll use to print it—a .TXT extension will hep you tell it from your other documents—exit back to the Print menu, and select Full Document. The document that's "printed" will be a disk file that you can take to another computer and print by using the PRINT command.)

See "Printing" for more information about printing with DOS.

▶ **Tip:** *You can't usually PRINT a file that you've created with your word processing program. It has all sorts of codes in it that DOS knows nothing about.*

▶ **Tip:** *Printing to disk isn't the same thing as saving to disk or printing from disk!*

▶ **Tip:** *Another way to PRINT a file is to copy it to your printer (PRN), like this: COPY file PRN:.*

Use PROMPT to change the DOS prompt (the A>, B>, C>).

PROMPT

PROMPT *options*

How to Enter It

Options

   $ special character used with options
   - starts a new line
   b produces | (a bar)
   e produces the Esc character
   h produces a backspace
   g produces > (greater than)
   l produces < (less than)

n produces the current disk drive
p produces the path
q produces = (equals)
t produces the time
v produces the DOS version number

Examples　**PROMPT pg** produces a prompt that shows you the current path to whatever directory you're in. (This is the most common use of PROMPT, and DOS 5 puts it in your AUTOEXEC.BAT file for you.)

PROMPT $t produces a prompt that shows the current time (as in 10:28:07.34).

PROMPT $p&_You called, master? displays the path, starts a new line, and presents the message "You called, master?".

Details　Use the PROMPT command in your AUTOEXEC.BAT file to customize the system prompt however you like it. You might want to use your name instead of the "master" in the example.

To go back to the default prompt, C>, just type PROMPT at the prompt.

QBASIC　Use QBASIC to start Qbasic, a programming language utility that comes with DOS 5.

How to Enter It　**QBASIC filename** *options*

Examples　**QBASIC MYPROGRAM.BAS /EDITOR** starts QBasic, opens the file MYPROG.BAS, and starts the DOS Editor

Details　There are several options that control how you see in QBasic on your screen: /H displays as many lines of text as your monitor can; /B displays text in black and white, even if you have a color monitor; /NOHI lets you use a monitor that doesn't provide high-intensity video; and /G updates a CGA (color graphics) monitor as fast as possible. There's also a /MBF switch that makes QBasic treat IEEE-format numbers as Microsoft format numbers.

▶ **Tip:** *QBasic has online help. Just press F1 while you're in QBasic to get it.*

Teaching QBasic is more than we can do in this book, as you might have guessed.

Use RECOVER to try to recover a file if you get a message that DOS can't read the file.

RECOVER

RECOVER filename

How to Enter It

RECOVER LETTER.DOC attempts to recover the LETTER.DOC file in the current directory.

Examples

RECOVER C:\DOCS\LETTER.DOC recovers the LETTER.DOC file in another directory.

▶ **Tip:** *Don't try to recover executable (program) files. Just recover text files.*

RECOVER A: recovers the files on the disk in drive A.

If you get a message that DOS can't read a file or a disk, you can try using RECOVER. What you recover, though, will be named FILE001.REC, and so forth, so you'll have to look at what's in it (use TYPE) and then give it a meaningful name (use REN). Also, something (the part that was bad) will be missing from the file, so recovering an executable program file isn't of much use. You can recover text files, though, and use your word processing program to fill in the missing text, if you can figure out what it is.

⚠**Warning:** *Don't RECOVER *.*. This will turn all the files on the disk, even perfectly good ones, into sequentially numbered thingies. Specify only the files you want to recover.*

Other utilities that you can buy, like the Norton Utilities, are much more useful for recovering damaged files than RECOVER. Or you can try UNDELETE (for deleted files) or UNFORMAT (for formatted disks) instead.

Use RD (or RMDIR) to remove an empty directory from your filing system.

RD (RMDIR)

RD directory name

How to Enter It

RD C:\DOCS\LETTERS removes the subdirectory LETTERS.

Examples

Before you can delete a directory, it has to be empty of everything except the two files represented by . and .. .

REN Use REN (or RENAME) to give a file a new name.

How to Enter It **REN oldname newname**

Examples **REN LETTER1 LETTER2** renames the LETTER1 file as LET-TER2.

REN *.DOC *.TXT renames all files ending in .DOC in the current directory to end in .TXT. LETTER1.DOC becomes LETTER1.TXT, LETTER2.DOC becomes LETTER2.TXT, and so forth.

Choose Rename from the File menu.

REN C:\DOCS\LETTER.DOC COMDEX.DOC renames the file LETTER.DOC in the DOCS directory to be COMDEX.DOC. Note that you don't give a path with the new name.

Details Here's a command that really lets you put wildcards to work. You can rename big bunches of files at a time with wildcards in both the old names and the new names.

For example, suppose you wanted to rename a lot of files named SCREEN01, SCREEN02, SCREEN03, and so forth, as FIGURE01, FIGURE02, FIGURE03, and so forth. You could do that all with one command, as REN SCREEN?? FIGURE??. You could even change the extension at the same time. Say your SCREEN files had different extensions, like SCREEN01.CAP, SCREEN02.TIF, and so forth. Using REN SCREEN??.* FIGURE??.ART would give all those files an .ART extension.

▶ **Tip:** *You can't move a file into another directory with REN. You have to COPY it instead and then delete the original. Or use the Shell's Move command.*

If you're trying to use wildcards to rename a bunch of files and keep getting the "Duplicate file name or File not found" message, there's already a file with (at least) one of those names in that directory. Figure out which one it is (get a directory listing) and rename that file TEMP; then rename the rest of the files; then rename the TEMP file to whatever you wanted it to be.

▶ **Tip:** *Don't rename files with names that a program doesn't expect to find. WordStar looks for .WSD files, Lotus looks for .WKS files, and so forth.*

REN doesn't erase the original file; it's still there on disk, under its original name.

Use REPLACE to update files with their newer versions.

REPLACE file1 file2 *options*

REPLACE A:*.TXT C:\DOCS /A adds any new .TXT files that are on a floppy disk in drive A but not in the directory named DOCS on drive C to that directory. (The /A says "add files.")

REPLACE A:*.* C:\ /S searches all the subdirectories on drive C and replaces all the files that match the files on the disk on drive A. The /S says "replace files with the same names."

REPLACE DOCS\MEMO LETTERS /U replaces the MEMO document in the LETTERS directory with the MEMO document in the DOCS directory if it's a more recent version than the one that is already in the LETTERS directory. The /U says "replace just updated files."

This is a command that you probably won't use very often. It's mainly used when you get a disk with more recent versions of files that you already have on your hard disk. For example, you might get a set of updated printer drivers to use with a word processing program. Most software manufacturers usually supply an Update or Install program to automatically replace the old versions of the files with the new ones, though.

Note that you don't give the a file name, just a directory name, as the target; REPLACE searches for file names that match. Use the /A option if you want to add files that are on the source disk (the new one) but not in the directory on your hard disk.

There are a couple of other options you can use: /P to be prompted before each file is replaced, /R to replace only read-only files, and /W to wait for you to insert a floppy disk.

REPLACE

How to Enter It

Examples

Details

RESTORE

Use RESTORE to restore files that you've backed up with BACKUP.

How to Enter It

RESTORE drive with backups destination drive *options*

Examples

Choose Restore Fixed Disk from the Disk Utilities.

RESTORE A: C: /S restores all the backed-up files on a floppy disk in drive A onto the hard drive (C) back into their original subdirectories. The subdirectories will be created if they've been deleted. (The /S restores subdirectories.) The directory you backed up from should be your current directory on drive C; otherwise, give the directory name and the *.* specification for "all files."

RESTORE A: C:\DOCS*.* /P restores files on a disk in drive A to the DOCS directory on drive C and prompts you if it finds a file on drive C that was changed after the backup. (The /P is for prompt.)

RESTORE A: C: /M restores only the files on the disk in drive A that have been modified since the last backup.

RESTORE A: C: /A:02-16-92 restores only files that have been changed on or after February 16, 1992. Using /B:02-16-92 would restore only files that were changed before that date.

Details

⚠**Warning:** *You can't change the name of a file when you restore it. Use the same name it was backed up under.*

If you don't specify a destination, RESTORE restores files into your current directory. If that directory isn't the same one that you used when the files were backed up, you'll get a message saying no files were found to back up. You don't want that, so be sure to specify a destination and a *.* for "all files."

You can change the drive letter, though. For example, you can restore files backed up from C:\SPREADS to D:\SPREADS.

Be sure to restore files in the same order they were backed up. That's why you marked those disks as 01, 02, and so forth (see BACKUP).

One other option, /N, restores files that aren't on the target disk any more (those that have been deleted since the last backup). This is handy to use if you're worried about restoring older files onto newer ones.

There are also time options that you can use.

/E:HH:MM:SS restores files that were modified on or before the specified time, and /L:HH:MM:SS restores files that were modified on or after that time. But be warned: using the time without a date can give you some very weird results!

If it's been a while since you made the backup, you may have edited some of the files on the hard disk, and they'll be a more recent version than the ones on the backup disks. If you think that might be the case, use the /P option so that you'll be prompted if DOS finds a more recent file on drive C.

▶ **Tip:** *You can't work with a backed-up file unless you've restored it to your hard disk.*

SHARE is used if you're working on a network to set up file sharing.

SHARE

SHARE *options*

How to Enter It

This one is best left to your network administrator. It sets up your system to allow file sharing.

Details

Some program installation procedures don't like to SHARE. You may get strange messages. PageMaker won't recognize its own installation disks, for example. (Maybe they'll have fixed this by now, though.) To get around it, start your computer with a startup disk in drive A (see the FORMAT entry for how to do this).

Use SORT to alphabetize lines in a file..

SORT

SORT *options*

How to Enter It

SORT < CLIENT.DOC sorts each line in the file CLIENT.DOC alphabetically and displays the results on the screen.

Examples

SORT < CLIENT.DOC > PHONE.DOC sorts each line in the CLIENT.DOC file alphabetically and puts the results in a file named PHONE.DOC.

SORT /+25 < CLIENT.DOC sorts the CLIENT.DOC file alphabetically beginning at position 25, so if last names began at that position (if the text were in regular columns), the file would be sorted by last name.

SORT < CLIENT.DOC /R does a reverse sort (one in which z is first).

Details   SORT is one of those redirection commands that make you use the < and > symbols. If you leave out the <, your file won't get sorted.

SORT thinks numbers are characters and sorts them one by one. This can cause problems because it will sort as if 11 comes before 2. (Use leading zeroes like 02 to get around this.) It also doesn't recognize tabs, so if your file has tab spaces in it, the results may not be what you think.

It's usually better to use a word processing program or database that has a sophisticated sorting routine, like WordPerfect or Microsoft Word, to sort files.

SUBST   Use SUBST to set up shorthand notation for long directory names.

How to Enter It   **SUBST drive: path**

Example   **SUBST E: C:\WORD\DOCS\LETTERS\JONES** lets you type E: instead of C:\WORD\DOCS\LETTERS\JONES to refer to the JONES subdirectory.

Details   If you find yourself frequently having to type out long paths to a directory, you can set up a shorthand notation for them with SUBST. You can use drive D: or E: as a replacement for the long path names. (If you want to use other letters, you'll need to use the LASTDRIVE command in your CONFIG.SYS file to tell DOS what your last drive letter is, because it only knows about A through E.)

Like ASSIGN and JOIN, SUBST fools DOS into thinking one thing is actually another. Be careful not to use commands that require DOS to really know what's what, like BACKUP and RESTORE, while SUBST is in effect.

To remove a substitution, type SUBST followed by the substituted drive and a /D, as in SUBST E: /D for the example above.

To see what substitutions you've set up, type SUBST.

Use SYS to make a disk that you can use for starting your system.

SYS DRIVE:

SYS A:

The SYS command puts hidden operating system files on a disk so that you can use it as a startup disk. If you have a laptop that runs from floppies, you may need to use this one from time to time.

Instead of using the SYS command, use FORMAT /S. It will format the disk, put the system files on it, and copy COMMAND.COM on it so that you don't forget to.

Normally you'll use SYS on a blank disk. With DOS 4 or later, you can use a disk that already has files on it, assuming there's enough room on it for your system files.

▶ **Tip:** *You'll also need to copy the file COMMAND.COM onto the disk; SYS doesn't copy it automatically for you.*

Use TIME to see the current time or to set the system time for the current session.

TIME displays the current time.

TIME hh:mm:ss sets the time without prompting you.

TIME 8:30p sets the time to AM/PM format.

You'll probably want to change the time at least twice a year for Daylight Savings time. But to set the time "permanently," you need to use a separate utility program (mine's called SETCLOCK) that came with your system clock.

If you don't want to set the time, just press Enter after you're prompted for a new time.

If you don't have an AUTOEXEC.BAT file, you'll be prompted for the date and time each time you start your computer. Good reason to set one up if you don't have one already.

TREE   Use TREE to get a graphic display of your file structure.

Examples   **TREE C:** shows you the directories and subdirectories of the files on drive C:.

TREE /F lists the files in the directories, too.

▶ **Tip:** *If you just want to find a file somewhere in your subdirectories, use DIR /S. It's faster than TREE.*

TREE /A uses an alternate character set that's a little fancier than the regular one (new in DOS 4).

**TREE ** shows you the directory structure starting at the root directory.

Details   If you get lost in your filing system, you can use TREE to get an idea of how your directories are set up.

If you have a lot of directories, they will zip by pretty quickly. Use TREE | MORE to see long directory trees.

TYPE   Use TYPE to see the contents of a text file on the screen.

How to Enter It   **TYPE filename**

Examples   **TYPE READ.ME** shows the contents of a file named READ.ME in the current directory.

TYPE READ.ME | MORE displays the file one screen at a time.

Details   When you buy a program, you'll often get a README file with it explaining last-minute changes and so forth. You can read these files before you start the program by using the TYPE command.

Press F9 to see what's in a highlighted file.

Use TYPE only with text files. If you use it on a program file (one that ends in .EXE or .COM), you'll just see garbage on the screen.

▶ **Tip:** *You can also use Ctrl-S to stop scrolling and Ctrl-Q to start it again.*

If the file is longer than one screen of text, use the MORE trick in the example above, or use the command as MORE < READ.ME.

Use UNDELETE to get deleted files back.

UNDELETE filename *options*

UNDELETE recovers all deleted files in the current directory one at a time.

UNDELETE C:*.DOCS /ALL undeletes all files in the root directory of drive C that end in .DOC.

UNDELETE /LIST lists the files that can be undeleted

UNDELETE /ALL recovers all deleted files without prompting you

UNDELETE A:OLDFILE undeletes the file named OLDFILE on the disk in drive A.

⚠**Warning:** *Undelete can't recover deleted directories. And it can't recover a file if you deleted the directory that contained it.*

Use UNDELETE as soon as you realize you've deleted a file by mistake! If the file's been written over by another file, you won't be able to get it back.

If you've installed MIRROR and you get a message saying DOS can't find anything to undelete, try entering *undelete /dos.*

 *Choose Undelete from the Disk Utilities.*

Use UNFORMAT to restore a disk that you've formatted by mistake.

UNFORMAT drive *options*

UNFORMAT A: unformats the disk in drive A.

UNFORMAT A: /TEST or **UNFORMAT A: /J** test to see whether the disk in drive A can be unformatted.

UNFORMAT A: /P gives you a printed copy of the UNFORMAT process (turn your printer on first!).

UNFORMAT C: /PARTN rebuilds your hard disk partition if it's been destroyed, if you've used the MIRROR command with the /PARTN option to put the partition information on a floppy disk (see MIRROR). After you give this command, you'll need to restart your computer with a DOS startup disk in drive A and then give the UNFORMAT command without the /PARTN option.

Details

This handy new command restores a disk to the way it was before you formatted it. If you need to use it on a hard disk, you'll have to start your system from a floppy disk in drive A. That disk should have a CONFIG.SYS file on it so that DOS can tell what devices you're using. The Uninstall disk created when you installed DOS 5 will do.

▶ **Tip:** *You can't unformat a disk that's been unconditionally formatted (with FORMAT /U).*

You should also have used the MIRROR command, ideally in your AUTOEXEC.BAT file, so that DOS has an up-to-date record of what was on the disk. See MIRROR.

VER

Use VER to see the version number of DOS you're using.

How to Enter It   **VER**

Details

Why would you need to know this? Well, you might be at somebody else's computer and not know which version of DOS was on it. DOS 4 and 5 have commands that version 3.3 doesn't have.

VERIFY

Use VERIFY to make sure that files are written on the disk correctly, especially when you're making copies.

How to Enter It   **VERIFY ON, VERIFY OFF**

Details

▶ **Tip:** *The shorthand for VERIFY is not VER. That's a different command. There's no shorthand for VERIFY.*

If VERIFY is on, all disk writing operations, like saving a file, will be double-checked automatically. You may want to put VERIFY ON in your AUTOEXEC.BAT file, but it does slow down your hard disk a little.

You can also use COPY or XCOPY with the /V option instead of turning VERIFY on.

Use VOL to see the volume label on a disk. **VOL**

VOL A: shows the volume label of the disk in drive A:. **Example**

If you've used the LABEL command to make a disk label, **Details**
you can see what that label is by using VOL, or see that
there's no label at all on the disk, which is perfectly OK,
too. Using volume labels is completely optional.

You'll also see a volume serial number, which I've never
found any good use for. Maybe if you have, you could
write me and tell me, along with who wrote that great line
that opens this chapter.

Use XCOPY for copying files or whole directories and **XCOPY**
subdirectories.

XCOPY source file or **directory target file** or **directory** **How to Enter It**
options

XCOPY C:\DOCS A: copies all the files in the DOCS direc- **Examples**
tory onto a disk in drive A. Adding a /V after the A:
verifies each copy.

XCOPY C:\DOCS A: /S /E copies all the files in the DOCS
directory, plus any subdirectories that may be under it,
even if they are empty, to a disk in drive A. (/S copies all
subdirectories of the directory you specify, but not empty
subdirectories, and /E copies even empty subdirectories,
preserving the original structure.)

XCOPY C:\DOCS A: /P prompts you before each copy is ▶ **Tip:** *Notice that you put*
made. *your options after the*
target.

XCOPY A: C:\REPORTS copies all the files on the disk in
drive A to a directory named REPORTS on drive C. If the
REPORTS directory doesn't exist, XCOPY creates it at the
root directory.

XCOPY C:\DOCS A: d:02-16-92 copies only files that have
been changed on or after February 16, 1992.

XCOPY C:\DOCS A: /S /A is a little tricker. If you've used

▶ **Tip:** *This is how to rename a directory: XCOPY it to a new directory name; then delete everything in the original directory and remove it. It's easier to delete a directory in the Shell.*

the BACKUP command, only the files in the DOCS directory and its subdirectories that have been changed since you used it will be copied. This is a good way to make an incremental backup, assuming that you've made a complete backup earlier—only files that you've worked with will be copied. The /A copies only files that have been changed since the last time you used BACKUP or XCOPY with the /M option (see below).

▶ **Tip:** *Use this option to do incremental backups.*

XCOPY C:\DOCS A: /S /M is even more tricky. It tells DOS to copy the files in the DOCS directory and its subdirectories that have been changed (modified) since you last backed up, but also to tag the file so that it won't be copied the next time you do a BACKUP unless the file's been changed. Practically speaking, this means that you can use XCOPY instead of BACKUP to keep your files up to date (see Details).

Details

XCOPY gives you a couple of advantages over COPY. For one thing, it lets you preserve your directory structure if you use the /S option to copy entire subdirectories and the /E option to copy them even if they don't have any files in them.

▶ **Tip:** *You can use wildcards with XCOPY.*

So when should you use XCOPY? Well, just about any time you'd use COPY. XCOPY's a little faster. Also, if you're copying whole directories and their subdirectories, XCOPY is the best choice.

Use BACKUP if you're backing up your hard disk onto floppy disks. The disadvantage to using BACKUP ius that you can't work with the individual files on your backup disks; you have to use RESTORE instead and restore them to the hard disk in the order they were backed up before you can work with them again.

▶ **Tip:** *You can't use unformatted disks with XCOPY. Have a supply of formatted disks on hand before you begin.*

The bottom line? Most folks find that making backups with XCOPY is less cumbersome than using BACKUP. If you work with only a few files each day, you'll probably find XCOPY easier to use to make backups than BACKUP. How to do this? First, put your backup disk in drive A; then, for example, if you've worked in the \WP51 directory, you'd give the command as XCOPY C:\WP51 A: /S / M. Only the files you've worked with will be copied, so you'll keep the number of backup disks down.

Installing DOS 5

DOS 5 comes with a special installation program called Setup. You need to use it to upgrade to DOS 5; you can't just copy what's on the installation disks onto your hard disk, because what's on those disks is in a compressed format.

The Setup program will automatically check to see what kind of hardware you have and will ask to you verify what it finds.

To use the Setup program, if your computer's running and you already have a version of DOS on it, put Disk 1 in drive A (or B) and close the drive door. Type *A:* (or *B:*) and press Enter to make that drive current. Then type *setup* and press Enter. You'll see instructions on the screen for each step to take, and you can press F1 to get online help.

Early in the Setup program, you'll be asked to provide either two regular-density floppy disks or one high-density floppy disk. They don't have to be formatted. You'll be asked to label them "Uninstall 1" and "Uninstall 2."

Also early in the Setup program, you'll be asked whether you want to back up your hard disk. Don't panic! You don't *have* to back up your hard disk before installing DOS 5; it leaves your files intact and just changes DOS itself. What that option is there for is that in a very few cases, some people may have to repartition their hard disk because there's not enough room for DOS 5 (you need at least 2.8 Mb for DOS 5, but most folks can delete enough files to make enough room). Repartitioning *does*

> **Tip:** *If there's no previous version of DOS on your computer, you'll need to use a different set of disks labeled OEM VERSION. Call your computer dealer to get these disks.*

> **Tip:** *If you're using any pop-up programs (also called TSRs) like SideKick, turn them off before you install DOS.*

erase files, so that's why you get a backup option. You'll also be asked whether you want DOS to start up with the Shell or not. It's preset not to, but if you're new to DOS, you'll be better off choosing Yes. The Shell's a lot easier to use than the command line.

Floppy Disks

If you want to put DOS 5 onto floppy disks instead of onto your hard disk, you'll need seven 5.25-inch disks or four 3.5-inch disks. They don't have to be formatted; the Setup program will format them for you.

If you're using 5.25-inch disks, label them:

> Startup
> Support
> Shell
> Help
> Basic/Edit
> Utility
> Supplemental

If you're using 3.5-inch disks, label them:

> Startup/Support
> Shell/Help
> Basic/Edit/Utility
> Supplemental

Follow the same directions as above, but type *setup /f* instead of just *setup*.

You'll probably want to make backup copies of your DOS disks as soon as possible, by using the Disk Copy utility or the DISKCOPY command. See the Backup chapter for details

Network Installation

If you're installing DOS 5 onto a network, you may need to upgrade a file or two or take an extra step before you can install it. This is true for certain versions of these networks: Microsoft LAN Manager, 3Com 3+Open, H-P LAN Manager, DEC PATHWORKS and PCSA, Banyan VINES, DEC 10Net, ArtiSoft LANtastic, Farallon PhoneNet Talk, IBM PC LAN and IBM DOS LAN Requester, NCR LAN Manager, Novell NetWare, Olivetti Olinet-LM, and Ungermann-Bass Net/One LM. If you don't have a DOS manual (it lists each step in detail), call Microsoft or your network vendor to see what you need to do. In some cases you'll need a new file that's supplied by the manufacturer of the network software.

Details

The Setup program will change lines in your AUTOEXEC.BAT and CONFIG.SYS files so that DOS 5 will work properly. If it can't change those files for some reason, it will create new AUTOEXEC.BAT and CONFIG.SYS files and rename your old ones with a numeric extension, like AUTOEXEC.1. If for some reason you need to see what was in these files before you installed DOS 5, this information will help you find them.

Setup will keep your old version of DOS and save it in a directory named OLD_DOS.1. You can use the Uninstall disk that was created during setup to return to this version of DOS if you ever have to. You can also use this Uninstall disk as an emergency startup disk in case something happens to your hard disk. To start your computer with it, put the Uninstall 1 disk in drive A and turn on your computer (or press Ctrl-Alt-Del to restart it).

Oh, No! A Disk Error!

You may get a disk error message while Setup uncompresses files and copies them onto your hard disk. This can happen if there's a bad spot on your hard disk or one of your floppy disks. If this happens, try running Setup again.

If all the files except just a couple get uncompressed and copied, here's how to uncompress them manually and get them onto your hard disk (this happened to me with DOSSHELL, which is a very important file).

You can tell which files are compressed on the floppies; they're identified by a _ at the end of their name. For example, DOSSHELL.EX_ identifies the compressed DOSSHELL file. There's a utility (which thankfully is *not*

▶ **Tip:** *See the AUTOEXEC.BAT and CONFIG.SYS chapter if you need more information about what these special startup files do.*

▶ **Tip:** *Once you've installed DOS 5, don't start your computer with a startup floppy disk from a previous version of DOS. Use the Uninstall disk instead.*

compressed) called EXPAND.EXE that will let you set these compressed files free. It's on either Disk 2 or Disk 3, depending on whether you're using 5.25-inch disks or 3.5-inch disks.

Once EXPAND.EXE is on your hard disk, you can expand a compressed file that's on a disk in drive A like this:

EXPAND A:DOSSHELL.EX_ C:\DOS\DOSSHELL.EXE

Just remember to give the whole name (.EXE or whatever) at the end, in place of the _.

Oh, No! It Won't Start!

In a pinch, if your computer won't start from your hard disk after you've installed DOS 5, try this. Put the Uninstall 1 disk in drive A and restart your computer. When you get the Uninstall screen, type *e* to Exit. You can then look at your AUTOEXEC.BAT and CONFIG.SYS files and see if you can figure out what's causing the problem. (In the Shell, highlight each one and press F9 to see what's in it.) If you wind up calling Microsoft, they'll ask what's in your AUTOEXEC.BAT and CONFIG.SYS anyway.

If you forget and leave the Uninstall disk in drive A after you've installed DOS 5, your computer will automatically run the Uninstall program when it starts and you'll be asked whether you want to go back to a previous version of DOS. (If you do, you'll have to install DOS 5 again, if you want to use it.) Just type *e* to Exit unless you really want to uninstall DOS 5.

Oh, No! My Mouse Doesn't Work!

A very few mice won't work with DOS 5. But there's a README.TXT file on Disk 5 or Disk 3 (for 5.25 or 3.5-inch disks, respectively) that may tell you how to get around whatever's causing the problem.

Oh, No! It Won't Install!

OK, if you can't get Setup to work for you, here's the brute-force way to install DOS 5.

Install it onto floppy disks, following the directions above. Then put the disk labeled Startup into drive A and restart your computer with Ctrl-Alt-Del. Type these commands at the command prompt (press Enter after each line):

sys c:

copy command.com c:

c:

md dos

This will put the DOS system files on your hard drive (drive C) and create a directory named DOS. Then type

copy a:.* c:\dos*

This copies everything from the disk in drive A to your DOS directory. Take out the startup disk and, one by one, insert each disk into drive A and repeat the *copy *.* c:\dos* command.

Then type this at the DOS prompt (press Enter after each line):

ren autoexec.bat autoexec.old

ren config.sys config.old

This renames your current AUTOEXEC.BAT and CONFIG. SYS files so that you can use the new ones that come with DOS 5.

One last step: type these lines (press Enter after each one):

copy c:\dos\config.sys c:

copy c:\dos\autoexec.bat c:

del c:\dos config.sys

del c:\dos\autoexec.bat

This copies the new AUTOEXEC.BAT and CONFIG.SYS files and deletes the old ones.

Finally! Take the disk out of drive A and restart your computer. If this doesn't work, call Microsoft Technical Support for some more hints about what may be going wrong..

Index